Infantrymen go down the cargo net and into a boat for the Normandy landing.

COVER: *The first wave of marines swarms ashore on Bougainville Island in the Pacific. Men are already dropping, but the beach was taken and held.*

FRONT ENDSHEET: *Japanese bombers surprise the American fleet at Pearl Harbor on December 7, 1941. They got eight battleships and three cruisers.*

CONTENTS PAGE: *A wartime poster urges Allied unity in the face of the foe.*

BACK ENDSHEET: *General Douglas MacArthur (at microphone) looks on as General Yoshijiro Umezu signs the Japanese surrender document aboard the battleship U.S.S. Missouri in Tokyo Bay on the morning of September 2, 1945.*

*"A knowledge of the past prepares us for the crisis
of the present and the challenge of the future."*

JOHN F. KENNEDY
From his special foreword in Volume 1

THE AMERICAN HERITAGE
NEW ILLUSTRATED HISTORY
OF THE UNITED STATES

VOLUME 15
WORLD WAR II

By ROBERT G. ATHEARN
Professor of History, University of Colorado

CREATED AND DESIGNED BY THE EDITORS OF
AMERICAN HERITAGE
The Magazine of History

PUBLISHED BY
DELL PUBLISHING CO., INC., NEW YORK

CONTENTS OF THE COMPLETE SERIES

Foreword by JOHN F. KENNEDY
Introduction by ALLAN NEVINS
Main text by ROBERT G. ATHEARN

A COMPLETE INDEX FOR ALL 16 VOLUMES APPEARS IN VOLUME 16

CONTENTS OF VOLUME 15

CHAPTER 43

BACKGROUND FOR WAR

Americans were so engrossed in a major battle for economic survival during the 1930s that many of them found it hard to realize that Europe, once so remote, so safely distant, was now coming dangerously near.

The principal cause for alarm was the power politics of dictators Adolf Hitler and Benito Mussolini and the Japanese military. Mussolini had come to power in Italy in 1922, and for a time, many Americans were disposed to regard him well, as a man who brought order, who "made the trains run on time." Then, in 1935, he picked a quarrel with Ethiopia, a primitive kingdom whose armed forces used spears and muzzle-loading rifles, and the world waited to see what the League of Nations would do about the aggression. Although the United States invoked an arms embargo and the league imposed economic sanctions, Italy was not to be put off. France in particular was afraid that the pressure would drive Mussolini

As the United States went to war again for the second time in 24 years, Norman Rockwell did this painting of the American soldier from the time of the Revolution.

closer to Hitler. In a six-month campaign, Italy completed its conquest.

Japanese generals and admirals who had been making and breaking governments in their homeland since 1900 attacked and occupied Manchuria in 1931 and followed up the gain with a drive into China in 1933. The United States, struggling through the worst of the depression, stood by and did nothing despite the protests of Secretary of State Henry L. Stimson.

In Germany, Adolf Hitler, an Austrian who had been a corporal in the German army in World War I, had been attempting to seize power with his National Socialist Party since 1923. By 1933, a combination of Hitler's great oratorical ability, wide unemployment, and the business community's fear of the German Communist Party enabled him to emerge as chancellor. Five months later, war hero President Paul von Hindenburg was dead and Hitler was dictator of the nation. He immediately set about rearming Germany in spite of the terms of the Treaty of Versailles.

To many Americans, Italy's adventure in Ethiopia and Japan's in China seemed far away, but the boldness of

British Prime Minister Neville Chamberlain thought he had made "peace in our time" by giving Hitler the Sudetenland.

Hitler's moves was of much greater concern. His policy of violent anti-Semitism was cause for alarm throughout the Jewish community in the United States. His effective assistance to rebel General Francisco Franco in the Spanish Civil War, beginning in 1936, was proof of his growing power. In the same year, he remilitarized the Rhineland, against the advice of his own generals. France and Britain did nothing. Screaming that the German people wanted "guns instead of butter," he annexed Austria in 1938, chipped the Sudetenland off Czechoslovakia, and then took over the whole of that unhappy country in March, 1939. In September, 1938, Britain's Prime Minister Neville Chamberlain had gone to Munich, acquiesced in the Czechoslovakian seizure, and returned to London to announce, "I believe it is peace in our time."

Russia's Foreign Minister Maxim Litvinov worked hard for an alliance between his own country, Britain, and France against Hitler, but the French and English could not bring themselves to become partners with the Communists. Then, Russian dictator Joseph Stalin made his own non-aggression treaty with Hitler. Coming up with too little too late, Chamberlain made a unilateral guarantee to protect Poland, Hitler's next target. Hitler calculated that he could defeat Poland before England could act, and on September 1, 1939, struck with tanks, infantry, and Stuka dive bombers. Russia promptly attacked from the east, and before the month was out, a brave Polish army, which contained such anachronisms as lancer cavalry, collapsed. As Hitler had foreseen, the British and French declared war, but did little but sit behind France's supposedly impregnable Maginot Line.

America views the war

Official American reaction to the outbreak of hostilities in Europe was similar to that of 1914: The President proclaimed neutrality. On September 5, 1939, he said, "I hope the United States will keep out of this war. I believe that it will. And I give you assurances that every effort of your government will be directed toward that end." However, unlike Woodrow Wilson, Franklin D. Roosevelt did not ask the people to be neutral in thought as well as deed. He admitted that "even a neutral has a right to take account of the facts." By this attitude, he acknowledged that the situation was somewhat different from that of 1914. This time, American public opinion was heavily in favor of the Allies.

In Roosevelt's neutrality proclamation of September 5, he had declared an embargo on the shipment of arms to belligerents. Later that month, he called Congress into special session and asked for a revision of the existing neutrality laws. Congress responded by lifting the arms embargo, but it retained the prohibition of loans to belligerents. By this action, it attempted to do two things—first, to maintain America's traditional policy of shipping goods to any and all and, second, to stay free of involvement with one side similar to that of 1914–17 which, some people felt, developed from the policy of making loans to England. The act, passed on November 4, also barred United States ships from war zones and forbade American citizens to travel on the ships of belligerent nations. Memories of the Americans who died when the Germans torpedoed the British liner *Lusitania* in 1915 still haunted the legislators.

Nevertheless, an effort was made to help the Allies without entering into

Adolf Hitler was boss of the Rome-Berlin axis. His partner, Benito Mussolini, was sometimes called the Sawdust Caesar.

any military participation. The United States was willing to sell them goods provided it did not have to deliver them. This "cash and carry" policy put a tremendous strain on the British merchant marine, which, under effective attack from German submarines, lost approximately 3,000,000 tons of shipping during the first year of the war.

The Neutrality Act was the high point of American determination to stay out of the war. From that time on, the administration moved gradually toward the conviction that the conflict was a struggle to save democratic civilization and that the United States had a share of responsibility in it. Even in 1939, a good many Americans did not object to all-out aid short of war. A Gallup poll taken that fall showed that 62% of the people were in favor of helping the Allies by sending materials, while 84% picked them as likely winners. Only 2% favored the Germans, while 14% had no opinion. At that time, 5% of those polled favored an immediate declaration of war on Germany, and 29% were willing to take that course if Germany appeared to be winning.

American preparedness

Although Roosevelt, Assistant Secretary of the Navy in World War I, had been building up the fleet since the mid-'30s, further enlargement of all the armed forces was necessary, and to do it effectively would require a draft. This would not only be unpopular, it would also be unprecedented, for never in American history had there been peacetime conscription. Early in 1940, Senator Edward R. Burke (Democrat, Nebraska) and Representative James W. Wadsworth (Republican, New York) presented the bill to Congress. The bipartisan nature of the move was underscored when Wendell L. Willkie, Republican Presidential candidate, approved it in his speech accepting the nomination. The Selective Training and Service Act, approved September 16, 1940, called for the registration of all males between the ages of 21 and 35. Those "selected" were to serve for one year—in the Western Hemisphere only. On registration day,

October 16, 16,400,000 young men signed up with a minimum of protest. Tin Pan Alley quickly produced *Don't Worry, Dear, I'll Be Back In a Year.* By the time the year was almost over, it was rumored that the increasing gravity of the international situation might mean that many who were in the service would be kept on longer. In the training camps, latrines blossomed with the letters O.H.I.O., for "Over The Hill In October." But October passed and few servicemen went "over the hill" as deserters.

The fleet got a boost in July, 1940, with the passage of a billion-dollar appropriation designed to build a two-ocean navy and increase total tonnage by 70%. It also provided for a 15,000-plane naval air arm.

In May and June, the German *blitzkrieg,* or "lightning war," had swept through Belgium, Holland, and France. Those countries were occupied, and a badly battered British Expeditionary Force barely got home from the beaches around the French port of Dunkirk. During the summer of 1940, the great Battle of Britain was fought. The victory of the Royal Air Force over Hitler's bombers staved off a possible invasion, but it did not assure permanent immunity from Nazi attack.

Roosevelt took another step toward war in the fall of 1940. In exchange for 99-year leases on bases in Newfoundland, Bermuda, the Bahamas, Jamaica, British Guiana, Trinidad, and other smaller locations, he turned

Pinned against the sea at Dunkirk, 233,000 British and some 100,000 French troops were rescued by a pickup fleet of naval, merchant, and civilian craft.

over 50 World War I American destroyers to Great Britain. This was of great assistance militarily, but the British were in severe financial straits. If they were to continue their war effort, supplies from America could not be denied them.

Roosevelt's answer was "Lend-Lease." First, he sought and found a legal basis for what he was about to propose—in a law of 1892 that said the President could, through the Secretary of War, lend army property "not required for the public use" for a period up to five years. Then he went before the people in one of his radio "fireside chats" and explained the problem in a simple parable. "Suppose my neighbor's home catches fire, and I have a length of garden hose," he began. "Now what do I do? I don't say to him, 'Neighbor, my garden hose cost me $15; you have to pay me $15 for it.' What *is* the transaction that goes on? I don't want the $15; I want my garden hose

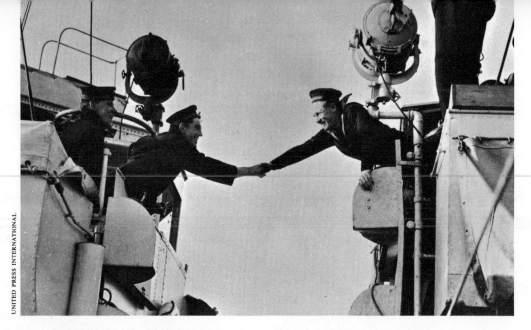

British sailors congratulate each other on arriving safely, after helping bring to England two of the 50 overage American destroyers lend-leased by Roosevelt.

back when the fire is over." Roosevelt then spelled out the parallel: Without American aid, Britain would go down and war would come to the American doorstep. "We must," he concluded, "become the arsenal of democracy."

From the beginning of American aid to the Allies there had been a numerically small but highly vocal opposition. It ranged from the Nazi-like members of the German-American Bund to pacifists—citizens who believed that wars were incited by munitions manufacturers and citizens who simply couldn't understand that the world had changed since George Washington warned against getting entangled in European affairs. From all these groups came an outcry against Lend-Lease. In Congress, Senator Burton K. Wheeler (Democrat, Montana) said it was "the New Deal's Triple-A foreign policy: it will plow under every fourth American boy." (This was a

reference to the Agricultural Adjustment Act of 1933, which provided for the curtailment of crop production to reduce surpluses.) Such prominent Americans as Herbert Hoover and Charles A. Lindbergh made speeches against the administration's program. Senator Robert A. Taft (Republican, Ohio), who had nearly won his party's nomination in 1940, went along with lend-leasing to Britain, but opposed giving anything to Russia, which Hitler, in violation of his treaty with Stalin, had invaded in June, 1941. Despite the protests from those who wanted to aid "America first" (and thus became known as America Firsters), the Lend-Lease Bill passed Congress with an initial appropriation of $7,000,000,000 to implement it.

Obviously, Roosevelt intended to go far beyond the law of 1892. America would order huge quantities of new equipment for shipment to Britain. To help solve the problem of getting it overseas, Roosevelt set up a "neutrality patrol," which was in fact nothing but an innocent-sounding name for a system whereby the United States Navy convoyed British shipping to an Atlantic midway point at which British escorts picked it up. To provide additional tonnage, the government seized 28 Italian and two German ships it had impounded early in the war. Thirty-five Danish vessels, caught in American ports when the Nazis overran Denmark, were taken over. The President obtained from the Danish minister in Washington (acting for his imprisoned king) the right to build air bases in Greenland. United States troops occupied Iceland. The bridge to Britain was almost complete.

Through the summer of 1941, the Germans drove deeply into Russia. At the same time in the Atlantic, their submarines, operating in "wolf packs," sent British shipping losses soaring so high that London stopped publishing the figures. Supplying the new ally, Russia, through its northern port of Murmansk was even harder than supplying Britain. Convoys bound there were exposed not only to submarines but also to surface ships and aircraft based in Nazi-occupied Norway. Some Americans distrusted Russia as an ally and agreed with Senator Wheeler when he said, "Just let Joe Stalin and the other dictators fight it out." Roosevelt, however, sent Harry Hopkins to Moscow to evaluate Russian intentions. The special envoy reported that he was convinced the Russians would not make a separate peace with Germany and that they should be strongly supported.

Diplomats at sea

Toward mid-August, 1941, Franklin Roosevelt and British Prime Minister Winston Churchill met off the Newfoundland coast in a historic conference. Aboard the American cruiser *Augusta*, the two men discussed the direction the war had taken and made plans to cooperate more extensively in stopping the Axis powers. Out of

Ohio Senator Robert A. Taft was a leading Republican exponent of isolationism but later voted for the United Nations.

Roosevelt and British Prime Minister Winston Churchill met on a ship at sea and drew up the historic Atlantic Charter, which stated their war aims.

the long conversations came a formalized set of principles that was to become known as the Atlantic Charter. In its eight points, many heard an echo of Wilson's Fourteen Points of 1918. First, it stated that neither the United States nor Great Britain sought aggrandizement. It went on to say that these powers hoped that after the war there would be no territorial changes not in accord with the wishes of the people concerned and that all people would have the right to choose the form of government under which they wished to live. Further, they looked for the closest cooperation between all nations, victors and vanquished, in the economic field—to the end that world living standards might be raised and that all might live free of fear and want. Finally, "All nations of the world, for realistic as well as spiritual reasons, must come to the abandonment of the use of force."

The first shots

The Germans could hardly be expected to sit by and watch American aid flow to England unimpeded. In May, the American freighter *Robin*

1272

Moor was sunk. Early September saw the United States destroyer *Greer* attacked by a submarine near Iceland, and later that same month, another freighter, the *L. C. White*, went down off Brazil. In mid-October, the destroyer *Kearny* was torpedoed near Iceland but not sunk, and then the U.S.S. *Reuben James,* another destroyer, was sunk in the same neighborhood with a heavy loss of life. Roosevelt said the German policy was one of "international lawlessness" designed to abolish freedom of the seas, but in all fairness, the United States could no longer, even by the most wishful thinking, be called a neutral. On September 11, the President announced that the time had passed when American ships and planes would wait until the Nazi U-boats attacked. Enemy submarines found within the United States defense zone were to be sunk on sight.

In addition, Roosevelt asked for repeal of several parts of the Neutrality Act—the prohibition against arming merchantmen; bans upon entry of American ships into combat zones; and the denial of belligerent ports to American vessels. While Congress was debating the changes, news of the torpedoing of the *Kearny* arrived. Within a few hours, the House approved the request by an overwhelming vote. There was sharp debate over the issue in the Senate, with isolationists attacking the bill, but when the

Japanese Special Envoy Saburo Kurusu, Secretary of State Cordell Hull, and Ambassador Kichisaburo Nomura met and conferred just before Pearl Harbor.

Reuben James was sunk, the measure passed the Upper House.

Relations with Japan

American relations with Japan had been deteriorating since the seizure of Manchuria and the China invasion in the early '30s. The United States refused to accept the Japanese position that she had special rights in China, and in 1939, Secretary of State Cordell Hull announced that a 1911 trade treaty with Japan would not be renewed. In the same year, a large new loan was made to China and an embargo was put on shipments of scrap iron and steel to Japan. In 1940, after the fall of France, Tokyo decided it was time to get on the Axis band wagon, and their ambassador to Berlin, Saburo Kurusu—who would later keep Cordell Hull talking while the Japanese fleet steamed toward Pearl Harbor—signed a military alliance with Germany and Italy. That year Japan also proclaimed a sort of Monroe Doctrine for Asia, declaring that the Orient should be a single economic sphere under Japanese influence.

In September, 1940, in spite of warnings from American Secretary of State Cordell Hull that further aggression would have most serious effects on American public opinion, the Japanese put pressure on the French, then lying helpless under the Nazi heel, for concessions in Indochina. The concessions were granted, and Japanese troops occupied the country. In 1941, similar pressures were put on Holland for Indonesia. Great Britain and the United States promptly froze all Japanese assets and intensified the existing economic blockade.

In Tokyo, General Hideki Tojo became prime minister and the army suppressed all opposition political parties. On November 11, Secretary of the Navy Frank Knox warned that conflict in the Pacific was a distinct possibility. Undersecretary of State Sumner Welles echoed the warning. In November, Japan sent Special Envoy Kurusu—who had signed with the Axis—to Washington to give the United States "a last opportunity to make amends for past aggressions." Secretary Hull complained that the Japanese words were far from peaceful, and he cautioned them not to bluff, for, he said, the United States would not. On Saturday, December 6, President Roosevelt cabled a personal message to Emperor Hirohito asking him to help preserve the peace.

Hull met with Kurusu and Japanese ambassador Kichisaburo Nomura on Sunday, December 7, to hear their response to Roosevelt's plea for peace. At a meeting that began at 2:20 p.m., the secretary was informed that Japan had rejected American overtures. The United States was accused of conspiring with other powers to curb the spread of Japanese influence in the Far East and of keeping alive difficulties between Japan and China. Greatly angered, Hull—a caustic Southerner—scolded his callers and labeled the charges "infamous falsehoods."

D–DAY

It was the late spring of 1944, and the Hitler empire, which once stood at the gates of Moscow and the doorway to Suez, had been shrinking. North Africa had fallen, Sicily was gone, the Italian mainland was conquered to Rome and beyond, and Italy was out of the war. The Russians were driving the Nazis from Red soil and at some points were into Rumania and Poland. In the west, though, the German still stood at the Atlantic Wall (above), waiting for the Anglo-American invasion from England. A debate was raging over the defense: Stop the enemy on the beaches or keep a mobile force inland to stop him after landing. Field Marshal Erwin Rommel said, "An attempt must be made to beat off the enemy landing on the coast and to fight the battle in a more or less strongly fortified coastal strip." Adolf Hitler cast his vote with the field marshal.

1275

ASSAULT: "AWAY ALL BOATS!"

IMPERIAL WAR MUSEUM, LONDON

Allied Supreme Commander General Dwight D. Eisenhower planned to drop his para-troopers (above) behind the German defenses and put his infantry ashore under mass bombing (below) and a naval bombardment. On June 5, the weather turned bad. Ike debated and decided: "How long can you hang this operation on the end of a limb? Give the order."

F.P.G.

NATIONAL MARITIME MUSEUM, GREENWICH, ENGLAND

H-Hour was 6:30 a.m. on June 6. In the hours before dawn, the warships (above, center) bombarded the beaches and the little landing craft circled before forming into the assault waves. The first men ashore took what shelter they could find behind the iron obstacles (below) that Rommel had built in the shallows to tear the bottoms from the landing craft.

NATIONAL GALLERY OF CANADA, OTTAWA

D–DAY

LUCK ON THE BRITISH BEACHES

The Germans had expected the landing farther north in the Pas de Calais area, which was closest to England, and Eisenhower had deceived them by bombing the site heavily. The ruse worked, tying down German troops, and on two out of three British beaches the men got ashore against second-rate enemy units. Larger landing craft carrying tanks and artillery rammed onto the beaches to give the infantry the weapons needed against the counterattack.

BAD LUCK ON OMAHA

On the Americans' Omaha Beach (below), the story was bloodily different. Unknown to Allied intelligence, a crack German outfit had been moved onto the bluffs covering the beach for coast-defense exercises. These veterans lay low in the shelling, then emerged to inflict casualties as high as 40% on the first units ashore. Officers lost their men in the confusion and made do with pickups. A lieutenant yelled at the men crouching in the shale, "Are you going to lay there and get killed or get up and do something about it?" General Omar Bradley confessed, "I reluctantly contemplated the diversion of Omaha forces to the British beaches."

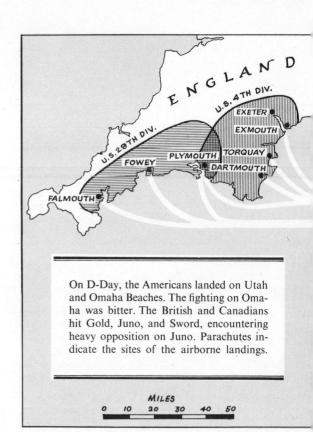

On D-Day, the Americans landed on Utah and Omaha Beaches. The fighting on Omaha was bitter. The British and Canadians hit Gold, Juno, and Sword, encountering heavy opposition on Juno. Parachutes indicate the sites of the airborne landings.

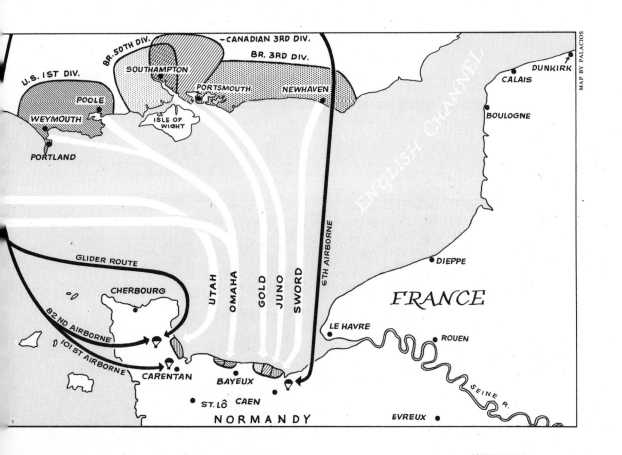

U.S. 1ST DIV.

BR. 50TH DIV.

SOUTHAMPTON

CANADIAN 3RD DIV.

BR. 3RD DIV.

POOLE

PORTSMOUTH

NEWHAVEN

WEYMOUTH

ISLE OF WIGHT

PORTLAND

DUNKIRK

CALAIS

BOULOGNE

ENGLISH CHANNEL

GLIDER ROUTE

CHERBOURG

82 ND AIRBORNE

101 ST AIRBORNE

UTAH

OMAHA

GOLD

JUNO

SWORD

6TH AIRBORNE

DIEPPE

FRANCE

LE HAVRE

ROUEN

CARENTAN

BAYEUX

SEINE R.

ST. LÔ

CAEN

EVREUX

N O R M A N D Y

MAP BY PALACIOS

COMBAT ART SECTION, U.S. NAVY

FOUL-UP AND SUCCESS ON UTAH

Both the British and American airborne landings were damp. Normandy is cut up with canals and overgrown creeks that Frenchmen call rivers. The British drop near the Orne and Dives Rivers (right) was designed to smash any bridges over which the Germans could bring up support, but to hold one bridge over the Orne by which commandos could come up to help them hold on. It went well. The American drops went badly in the hedgerows behind Utah Beach, but little groups of widely scattered jumpers (below, left) confused the defense. Many of them died in glider crashes or drowned in the marshes (below, right), but by early morning the key town, Ste. Mere-Eglise, had fallen and the Fourth Division driving in over Utah Beach had made it with only 197 casualties and had 20,000 men moving inland.

DEPARTMENT OF THE ARMY

TIME-LIFE COLLECTION, DEPARTMENT OF DEFENSE

NATIONAL GALLERY OF CANADA, OTTAWA

IMPERIAL WAR MUSEUM, LONDON

STRANGLEHOLD ON THE AIR

Rommel had advocated the tight defense on the beaches because he had learned during the North African campaign how air power could tie his panzers down. Now he wrote, "Our operations in Normandy are tremendously hampered by the immensely powerful, at times overwhelming, superiority of the enemy air force." Fighter-bombers (left) and rocket-firing fighters (above) closed the roads to his columns during daylight.

D-DAY

"TAKE THE MEN OFF THE BEACH!"

IMPERIAL WAR MUSEUM, LONDON

The British (above, left) were ashore and moving on toward Caen. Utah was in good shape, but on Omaha, casualties mounted (left). Acting as if he were bulletproof, American General Norman Cota strode the beach and shouted to "jar the men loose." It was 1:30 p.m. when Omar Bradley got the word "Troops advancing up heights behind the beaches" and German prisoners (above) began coming disconsolately back under guard.

THE DAY ENDS
IN VICTORY

They had done it. By the end of D-Day, a force of 200,000 men had come in over the beaches and three airborne divisions were causing havoc in the enemy rear. The casualties had been lighter than expected—about 10,000 for the job. Men of the First Division (above) pushed on inland, and infantry on ruined German bunkers waved to fighter-bombers (left) flying on to punish the German support. Today a cemetery and a monument (right) stand above Omaha Beach in memory of men who died for a 60-mile-wide part of Fortress Europe.

UNITED PRESS INTERNATIONAL

1289

FROM PEARL HARBOR TO BERLIN AND TOKYO

Even as Ambassador Nomura and Special Envoy Kurusu talked with Hull, the war had begun. A Japanese task force built around six aircraft carriers had been under way since November 26. About 2 p.m. on December 7, reports reached Washington that the carrier-based planes had launched a successful surprise attack on the United States Pacific Fleet at Pearl Harbor, Hawaii. The command at Pearl had been alerted for possible attack on November 27, but had failed to take appropriate action. There was little long-range reconnaissance; aircraft on the ground were not dispersed; vessels anchored along Battleship Row were not put to sea. Only by fortunate accident were the American carriers away on exercises. A radar operator picked up some pips and assumed them to be American bombers expected from the States.

The first wave of Japanese bombers and strafing fighter planes struck at 7:55 a.m., Hawaii time. On one cruiser,

The sea war in the Pacific was chiefly a battle between aircraft carriers. The American flattop Hornet fights for her life as a Japanese dive bomber crashes into her superstructure (upper right).

the Catholics in the crew had just left for Mass when the general-quarters—battle-stations—klaxon sounded. On the battleship *Oklahoma,* the public-address system blared, "Real planes, real bombs; this is no drill!" The Japanese pilots had already radioed back to their carriers, "Surprise attack successful." A second wave came over at 8:40 a.m., and when they were through, eight battleships and three cruisers were sunk or severely damaged, 347 aircraft were knocked out of action—most of them before they had a chance to leave the ground—and there were 3,478 American casualties.

On Monday, Roosevelt went before Congress and announced, "Yesterday, December 7, 1941—a date that will live in infamy—the United States of America was suddenly and deliberately attacked." Congress declared war and repeated the declaration on December 11, when Germany and Italy entered the war against the United States.

Simultaneously with the attack on Pearl Harbor there had been an equally successful attack on American forces based in the Philippines and lesser attacks on Wake and Midway Islands. Japanese land forces drove into Malaya and Thailand.

In spite of the disaster, for the first time in its history when it was not actually at war, the nation was at least partially prepared. Because of the peacetime draft, it had an army of 1,600,000 in various stages of training. When America entered World War I, she had an army of only 92,000. Before World War II was over, more than 15,000,000 men and women would serve in the armed forces.

War on far-flung fronts

One after the other, the Allied outposts in the Pacific fell—Guam, Wake Island, Hong Kong, Malaya, and the Philippines. The fight for the Philippines was bitter, with the forces of General Douglas MacArthur, badly outnumbered, forced to give ground until they were confined to the Bataan Peninsula and finally to the little island of Corregidor—"The Rock"—in Manila Bay. On May 6, 1942, Corregidor surrendered after MacArthur and a few of his staff had been evacuated to Australia by submarine on the order of President Roosevelt. The Japanese moved through the islands of the South Pacific so successfully that worried Americans feared Australia and New Zealand would be taken next.

During these gloomy days, military planners decided on a holding action against the Japanese—to keep them in check while aiming the main blows at Hitler's empire. It was a difficult choice, but Hitler and Mussolini controlled a vast industrial potential in Europe and their threat was, in the long run, greater than that in the East. The danger that Russia might fall before Nazi onslaughts—during the winter of 1941–42, the panzers were at the

In the Battle of the Coral Sea on May 7, 1942, American carrier planes turned back a Japanese force headed for Port Moresby. An American dive bomber pulls out after an attack on the Japanese carrier Shoho.

gates of Moscow—and thus give the enemy a large additional quantity of slave labor and industry deeply concerned the Allies.

Nevertheless, counterblows in the Pacific were quickly struck. By February, 1942, naval task forces built around the carriers that had escaped Pearl Harbor were hitting Japanese-held islands, and on April 18, 16 army medium bombers led by Colonel James H. Doolittle flew off two carriers to strike Tokyo and other Japanese cities. The material damage was minor, but the knowledge that their home islands were vulnerable hurt Japanese and raised American morale.

In May, the Japanese suffered their first real repulse. An American task force located an invasion force aiming for Port Moresby in New Guinea to cut the Australian supply line. The ensuing Battle of the Coral Sea was fought entirely between carrier-based planes—the first naval battle in history in which surface ships did not fire a single shot. The Japanese lost one carrier and had another damaged.

The Americans lost the *Lexington,* and the *Yorktown* was badly damaged. Most important, however, the invasion force was turned back. The Japanese spearhead had been blunted.

Much worse was shortly to come. Fleet Admiral Isoruku Yamamoto was convinced that the United States Pacific Fleet must be destroyed before the end of 1942. After that date, the reinforcements from American war production would make its strength overwhelming. To bring it to battle while the odds were still in his favor, Yamamoto planned to strike at Midway Island, the guardian outpost of Hawaii itself. Admiral Chester W. Nimitz, Commander in Chief of the Pacific Fleet, could not refuse battle. The Japanese had four big carriers and one light carrier against three for the Americans and an overwhelming superiority in battleships and cruisers.

In this seemingly hopeless situation, Admiral Nimitz had two advantages: His staff had succeeded in breaking the Japanese code and knew Yamamoto's plan in detail. One part of it was to send a small Japanese force into the North Pacific as a feint to draw the Americans out of position. Nimitz also had taciturn, grim-faced Raymond A. Spruance, called by Samuel Eliot Morison one of the greatest admirals in American naval history, in command of the carriers *Enterprise* and *Hornet.*

At 6 a.m. on June 4, a Midway patrol plane sighted the Japanese carriers. Admiral Frank Jack Fletcher, the senior officer present, ordered Spruance to head for them and launch his own aircraft as soon as he was within striking range. Fletcher himself would follow in the carrier *Yorktown* as soon as he recovered his search planes. In the meantime, the Japanese had bombed Midway once, but decided it needed another going over. Their planes were on the flight decks being refueled and rearmed when the first of Spruance's groups—the tor-

At Midway—the battle that doomed Japan—planes from three American carriers destroyed four Japanese carriers with the loss of only one American flattop.

Admiral Raymond A. Spruance, shown here during the Battle of Midway, later claimed modestly that all he did was get into action as quickly as possible.

pedo bombers—struck. The Japanese fighter cover and antiaircraft fire was too much for them, however. Only eight planes came out alive, and not a single torpedo found a target.

Torpedo planes come in low, and the Japanese triumph had disastrous final results. Their antiaircraft gunners had been watching the torpedo planes; their fighter cover was down close to the water. Two minutes after the last torpedo strike, American dive bombers arrived at 14,000 feet and were able to attack almost unopposed. First the *Akagi* got it, the bombs and fuel she was feeding her own planes bursting and burning to destroy her. Then *Kaga* took four hits and went down. *Soryu* went next, and only

Hiryu remained to strike back. She succeeded in damaging *Yorktown*, but moments later, an attack from *Enterprise* left *Hiryu* so damaged that she was finished off by her own destroyers. The battle that had begun with four big Japanese carriers against three Americans now stood at no Japanese against two Americans, and the tide of the war in the Pacific had turned for good. The force trying to take Midway limped home beaten.

The defense was now over, and in August came the first counterattack. The First Marine Division landed on Guadalcanal in the Solomon Islands and, aided later by army units, took the islands after a bitter six months' struggle. American battleships and

1295

American sailors operate a 1.1-inch anti-aircraft machine gun in the fierce fighting after the landings on Guadalcanal.

cruisers, still outnumbered by the enemy, had their finest hours of the war as they fought off Japanese surface units convoying reinforcements or coming down to bombard the crucial marine-held airfield.

The tide turns in Africa

Allied efforts to free the European continent began in North Africa, where German and Italian forces were threatening the Suez Canal. During the summer of 1942, Nazi General Erwin Rommel, "The Desert Fox," swept to within 70 miles of Alexandria, and the discouraged Allies were contemplating a retreat into the Middle East. Rommel was at the end of a long supply line, however, and the

British navy and air force were effectively interrupting it. In addition, General Bernard L. Montgomery's Eighth Army had been strengthened, mostly with shipments of American tanks. In October, 1942, his mixed force of British, Australians, New Zealanders, Indians, South Africans, and Free French attacked at El Alamein and sent Rommel reeling back toward Tunisia.

On November 8, an American force under General Dwight D. Eisenhower landed in French Morocco and Algeria, and the Axis troops were now pinched into Tunisia from two directions. Rommel was recalled to Germany, and on May 12, 1943, more than 250,000 Germans and Italians laid down their arms and the war in Africa was over.

Meanwhile, Roosevelt and Churchill met with their advisers at Casablanca and decided that the next move would be against Sicily to complete control of the Mediterranean before an attempt was made upon the European mainland.

On July 10, more than 3,200 vessels carried the American Seventh Army under General George S. Patton, Jr., and the British Eighth under Montgomery to Sicily. The American assignment was to secure the western half of the island, and this was done in a three-week campaign. The British were to drive up the east coast and capture Messina—the German escape port to the Italian mainland. The Germans concentrated heavily against Montgomery on ground favorable to the defense, and when the Allies finally entered Messina after more than six weeks' fighting, the Germans had got most of their troops and equipment out.

The fall of Sicily was also the fall of the long-tottering Benito Mussolini. On July 24, the Fascist Grand Council voted him out of office. A new government, under Marshal Pietro Badoglio, was then installed, and it signed an armistice in Sicily on September 3. But the Germans were not caught unprepared. They promptly disarmed the Italians—most of whom were delighted to quit the war in any way they could—and reinstalled Mussolini as a rival to Badoglio. Hitler intended to make the Allies fight for every foot of the mountainous peninsula.

The fight began September 3 when the Eighth Army jumped across the Straits of Messina and started up the Italian boot. Six days later, a British-American army under American General Mark Clark landed at Salerno and found itself in serious trouble. German Field Marshal Albert Kesselring had calculated that Salerno was exactly where the attack would come and had five divisions waiting for it on the rugged hills back of the beaches. For a desperate day, it seemed that the invaders might be thrown back into the sea, but Allied air power and naval gunfire prevailed, and by October 1, Clark's men were in Naples with the Eighth Army abreast of them

During the bitterly contested Salerno landings, a German Messerschmitt 109 fighter-bomber heads down in flames after a near miss on a landing craft.

Infantrymen tow a piece of artillery into position during the jungle fighting on New Guinea, where the swamps and disease held up MacArthur's advance.

to the east. Rome was only 120 miles away, but because of the defense put up by Kesselring in the mountains and a bitter, rainy winter that flooded the rivers and turned the front to mud, it would be June, 1944, before the Allies saw the Holy City.

Through Japan's outer defenses

Japan was now on the defensive, but it was a formidable defense, beginning with a string of island bases running from the North Pacific to the Solomons. Behind these lay another string of island outposts, including the bastions of the Philippines and Okinawa. All these had to be penetrated or bypassed before the heart, the Japanese home islands, could be reached.

The outer barrier was to be smashed in a three-stage attack based on a plan to get behind the most strongly defended positions, cut their supply line, and leave them unprovisioned and un-

supported. Thus, in the North Pacific, Kiska was bypassed and Attu taken in May, 1943, in a short, nasty fight in which almost the whole Japanese garrison of 2,350 were casualties.

At the southern end, the major Japanese base lay at Rabaul on New Britain Island. General MacArthur and a mixed American-Australian force were to advance from their base at Port Moresby and fight their way through the steaming jungles along the northern New Guinea coast. On the other side of Rabaul, Admiral William F. "Bull" Halsey's force was to take the islands of the northern Solomons, leaving the base flanked out on both sides.

MacArthur's men started struggling

The map shows the chief thrusts of the American counterattack in the Pacific. The vast distances made the supply problem one of the most difficult of the war.

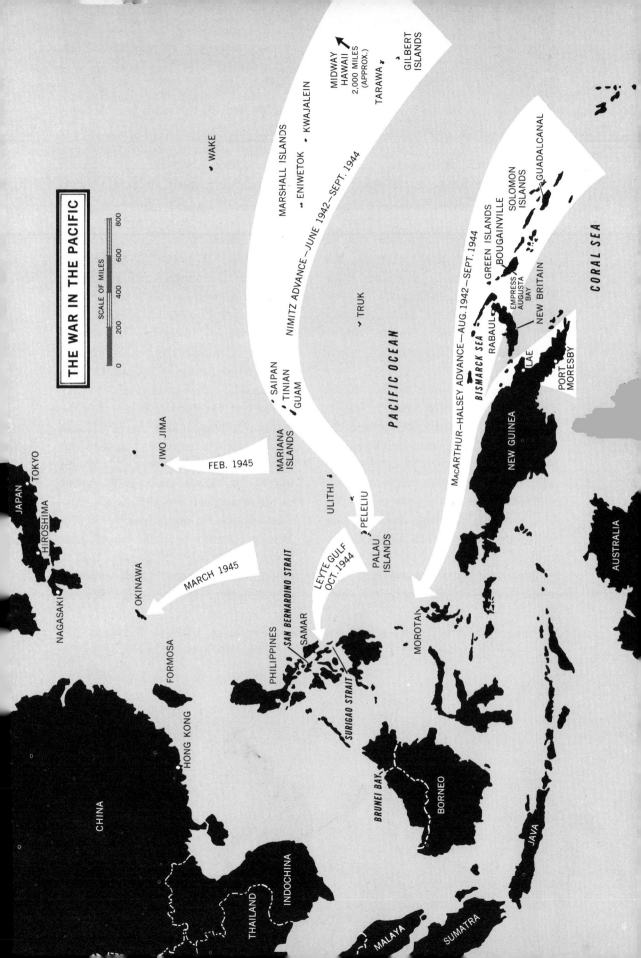

THE WAR IN THE PACIFIC

SCALE OF MILES

0 200 400 600 800

MIDWAY
HAWAII
2,000 MILES
(APPROX.)

GILBERT
ISLANDS

TARAWA

WAKE

MARSHALL ISLANDS

ENIWETOK • KWAJALEIN

NIMITZ ADVANCE—JUNE 1942—SEPT. 1944

TRUK

PACIFIC OCEAN

GUADALCANAL

SOLOMON
ISLANDS

BOUGAINVILLE

GREEN ISLANDS

EMPRESS
AUGUSTA
BAY

RABAUL

NEW BRITAIN

MacARTHUR–HALSEY ADVANCE—AUG. 1942—SEPT. 1944

BISMARCK SEA

LAE

PORT
MORESBY

CORAL SEA

SAIPAN
TINIAN
GUAM

MARIANA
ISLANDS

IWO JIMA

FEB. 1945

JAPAN

TOKYO

HIROSHIMA

ULITHI

PELELIU

PALAU
ISLANDS

LEYTE GULF
OCT. 1944

NEW GUINEA

AUSTRALIA

OKINAWA

MARCH 1945

NAGASAKI

SAN BERNARDINO STRAIT

SAMAR

PHILIPPINES

SURIGAO STRAIT

MOROTAI

FORMOSA

HONG KONG

CHINA

BRUNEI BAY

BORNEO

THAILAND

INDOCHINA

MALAYA

JAVA

SUMATRA

toward Lae in January, 1943. Tokyo promptly attempted to reinforce New Guinea with 20,000 troops carried in 12 transports convoyed by 10 warships. In the Battle of the Bismarck Sea, American and Australian planes caught the convoy and destroyed it with the loss of only four planes.

Even without reinforcements, the Japanese managed to keep MacArthur out of Lae until September. The jungle was their ally; the Americans lost nearly as many men to combat fatigue and malaria as they did to enemy bullets.

Working his way up the Solomons' ladder, Halsey ran into similar resistance from the island garrisons and the Japanese surface fleet. At Bougainville, the Americans attempted no direct assault on the Japanese garrison of 60,000 men, but simply grabbed a beachhead at Empress Augusta Bay with enough room for airfields that could be used against the rest of the island and against Rabaul itself, 210 miles away. Then, in February, 1944,

Halsey hopped to Green Island, completely cutting off Rabaul on its northern flank and putting American air power within 120 miles.

MacArthur, meanwhile, was leapfrogging along the northern New Guinea coast, making new landings to bypass heavy enemy concentrations in the jungle. By the end of May, 1944, he was at the western end of the island, the second largest in the world. Rabaul was finished as a base, and 135,000 Japanese troops were hopelessly stranded in the South Pacific.

The third prong of the attack was designed to seize enemy-held islands in the Central Pacific. Admiral Nimitz was in charge, and his first target was Tarawa, a tiny coral atoll in the Gilbert Islands. It turned out to be one of the bloodiest pieces of terrain in the whole war for the Americans. The admiral commanding the 4,000 Japanese troops on the island had fortified it heavily and boasted that it could not be taken with a million men. On November 21, the Second

Having received treatment from hospital corpsmen on the beach on D-Day, a wounded man is carried to a boat that will take him to a ship's sick bay.

Marine Division went ashore, after a naval and air bombardment, to see if the admiral was right. At first it seemed he was. Landing craft grounded on coral reefs, leaving the marines with 700 yards of Pacific to wade through to get ashore. The entire distance was under enemy fire because the heavy bunkers on the island had survived most of the bombardment. By the next morning, the marines had two small beachheads and one of their commanders messaged, "Our casualties heavy. Enemy casualties unknown. Situation: We are winning." After four days, they did win, but it cost nearly 1,000 dead and over 2,000 wounded. The experience was costly, but it taught Nimitz to insist on heavier bombardments and better landing craft in future operations. With lighter casualties, the marines and the army went on to take Kwajalein and Eniwetok in the Marshalls and Japan's outer barrier was gone.

The end of Fortress Europe

As 1944 opened in Europe, everyone knew what was coming. This was to be the year of the long-awaited cross-channel invasion for which British, American, Canadian, and French forces had prepared in England. Before it began, however, there was some unfinished business in Italy. "Smiling Albert" Kesselring had the Allies stalled in the mud along a line anchored on the fortress height of Monte Cassino. The decision was to outflank Kesselring by making a new

The Allied commander for the invasion of Europe was General Dwight D. Eisenhower.

landing behind him and cause him to pull back or be trapped between two forces. The spot chosen was Anzio, a small resort town in peacetime, just south of Rome. A force of 70,000 Americans and British got ashore easily on January 22, but failed to move inland quickly enough. The agile Kesselring held at Cassino and moved his reserves onto the hills above the beachhead. Far from threatening the Germans, the landing force just managed to hold on against hard counterattacks and then had to huddle in its dugouts, drummed by artillery fire from above. Not until May did the Fifth and Eighth Armies break through at Cassino, link up with the beachhead troops, and enter Rome, which the Germans had declared an open city and left, undamaged, on June 4.

Two days later—June 6, 1944—the

Hedgerows on embankments turned many Normandy fields into enemy forts that gave the American infantry stubborn resistance as it struggled to advance.

invasion of France finally came. In weather far from perfect, 150,000 men, 5,000 ships, and 12,000 planes set out over the choppy English Channel for the assault that was to free Europe. Just after midnight, British and American paratroopers started dropping behind the invasion beaches, and at 6:30 the seaborne forces went ashore at a series of points between Cherbourg and Le Havre. The paratroops and glider troops came down badly scattered and took heavy casualties. On Omaha Beach, two American divisions ran into ferocious opposition from a crack German unit stationed there, unknown to Allied intelligence, on anti-invasion maneuvers. The Canadians had hard fighting on Juno Beach, but in general the operation went well there, with casualties considerably lighter than had been feared.

Cherbourg was taken before the end of June, but breaking out of the beachhead proved a tough, slogging job with the British bogged down in front of Caen. Yet they tied up much of the German armor as the Americans pushed toward St. Lo through farmland where each small field was surrounded by an earthen bank and hedgerow that turned it into a little fort. It was near the end of July before the two forces had achieved their objectives. On July 26, the American First Army, aided by heavy bombing ahead of it, punched a clean hole through the German lines south of St. Lo and General Patton's tanks went roaring through to loop around toward Argentan, where they joined the Canadians and trapped most of two German armies. To add to the enemy's plight, on August 15, the American Seventh Army landed on the French Riviera against light resistance and drove rapidly north.

The map shows the assaults that finally destroyed the Third Reich. The tide turned in the fall of 1942, when the Nazi offensives failed in Russia and North Africa.

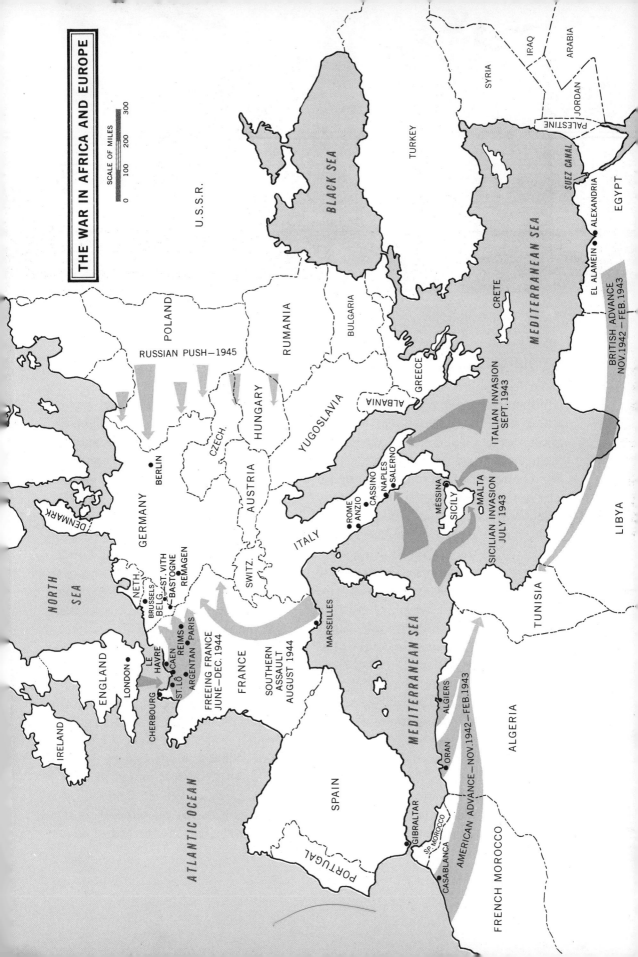

THE WAR IN AFRICA AND EUROPE

SCALE OF MILES

0   100   200   300

ATLANTIC OCEAN

IRELAND

ENGLAND
LONDON

NORTH SEA

DENMARK

NETH.
BRUSSELS
BELG.
ST. VITH
BASTOGNE
REMAGEN

GERMANY

BERLIN

POLAND

U.S.S.R.

RUSSIAN PUSH—1945

CZECH.

AUSTRIA

HUNGARY

RUMANIA

BULGARIA

BLACK SEA

TURKEY

LE HAVRE
CHERBOURG
CAEN
ST. LÔ
REIMS
ARGENTAN
PARIS

FRANCE

SWITZ.

YUGOSLAVIA

ALBANIA

GREECE

FREEING FRANCE
JUNE—DEC. 1944

SOUTHERN
ASSAULT
AUGUST 1944

MARSEILLES

ITALY

ROME
ANZIO
CASSINO
NAPLES
SALERNO

ITALIAN INVASION
SEPT. 1943

MESSINA
SICILY
MALTA

SICILIAN INVASION
JULY 1943

CRETE

MEDITERRANEAN SEA

SPAIN

PORTUGAL

GIBRALTAR

SP. MOROCCO

CASABLANCA

FRENCH MOROCCO

ALGIERS
ORAN

AMERICAN ADVANCE—NOV. 1942—FEB. 1943

ALGERIA

TUNISIA

MEDITERRANEAN SEA

LIBYA

EL ALAMEIN

ALEXANDRIA

EGYPT

SUEZ CANAL

BRITISH ADVANCE
NOV. 1942 — FEB. 1943

PALESTINE

JORDAN

SYRIA

IRAQ

ARABIA

This is a typical field-dressing station set up just behind the front in a ruined village church. From here, stretcher cases moved to the rear in jeeps.

Hitler's men streamed back to the Siegfried Line, a defense position just outside Germany itself. Paris was free after four years, and General Charles de Gaulle arrived during the three-day spree of jubilation.

On the Allied left flank, the English and Canadians also moved swiftly and were in Brussels and Antwerp, Belgium, by early September. Then enemy resistance stiffened. Montgomery tried to outflank the Siegfried Line by dropping one British and two American airborne divisions north of it and then breaking through with a British army to support them. The breakthrough failed, and the paratroopers had to fight their way back with heavy losses. The conflict settled down to hard fighting for small gains in increasingly bitter weather.

Hitler's last gasp

With the Russians driving in on him from the east, Hitler resolved to stake almost his total available re-serve in a final effort against the Allied ring in the west. If the attack could recapture the Channel ports, the Americans and British might be discouraged enough, he thought, to make a separate peace. The drive would be made in the Ardennes, a thinly held sector where four American divisions were occupying a 90-mile stretch of front. It was hoped that bad winter weather would keep Allied air power on the ground. To do the job, a force of 250,000 men and 2,000 tanks was scraped together and assembled in the greatest secrecy. On December 16, the startled Americans saw them come rolling forward through an early morning fog. The front collapsed, and before it could be reestablished, the Nazis had rolled through the snow to make a bulge 45 miles wide and 65 miles deep.

The Allied defense firmed, then began to drive in on the flanks of the bulge with strong air support as the weather cleared. By the end of January, the lines were right back where they had been when the fight started, and all Hitler had to show for the Battle of the Bulge were 90,000 casualties.

The death of the Third Reich

There was still fierce fighting ahead, even against the boys and old men Hitler now had to use to eke out his forces, but by mid-March the Allies were on the Rhine and over it at Remagen, where a bridge was taken before it could be destroyed. Then Montgomery got six divisions across in a combined paratroop and ground attack. Suddenly everybody was moving forward, the Ruhr was encircled, and 325,000 German troops surrendered. Through April, the Allies converged on Berlin from east and west. On April 28, Mussolini was shot by Italian partisans, and on April 30, Hitler committed suicide. Two days later, the Russian army entered Berlin. On May 7, General Alfred Jodl, representing what German government there was, signed an unconditional surrender in Eisenhower's headquarters at Reims. After almost six years, the war in Europe was at an end.

Closing in in the Pacific

The time had come for the assault on the islands close to Japan, and in June, 1944, Commander of the Pacific Fleet Nimitz sent Admiral Spruance after the key island of Saipan in the Marianas. Once it was taken, airfields could be built there from which the new B-29 bombers could attack Japan itself. Spruance had 77,000 men and the Japanese

Allied bombers regularly worked over German cities to reduce their war production capacities. Below are the ruins of Nuremberg after six years of war.

commander had 32,000, but the terrain was rugged and its defenders were stubborn. They fought for nearly a month, with the last Japanese units dying in wild banzai charges that piled in on American positions until marine and army artillerymen were firing with their fuses set on zero.

On June 19, the Japanese sent a carrier force down in an attempt to drive off the Americans. In the three-day air battle that followed, they lost over 300 planes and three carriers; the Americans lost only 23 Hellcat fighters. The score on land was not nearly so favorable; there were over 16,000 American casualties before the island was secured and the B-29s had their base. Guam and Tinian were captured after more heavy fighting, and the conquest of the Marianas was complete.

Farther south, MacArthur's men landed on Morotai Island, thus flanking the Philippines on that side, and Halsey took Peleliu in the Palau Islands after the bitterest kind of fighting. Now MacArthur could make good his promise to return to the Philippines.

The end of the Japanese navy

MacArthur was to land at Leyte Gulf on Leyte Island. To support him, there were two fleets—Halsey's Third, with the fast carriers to deal with any intervention by the Japanese navy, and Admiral Thomas Kinkaid's Seventh to provide fire support for the ground troops. Many of Kinkaid's battleships had been raised from the mud at Pearl Harbor where the raid that started the war had left them, and their moment of vengeance was now at hand.

To counter the landing, the Japanese had devised a complex and crafty plan. They had some carriers left, but a

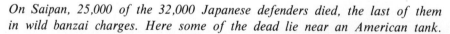

On Saipan, 25,000 of the 32,000 Japanese defenders died, the last of them in wild banzai charges. Here some of the dead lie near an American tank.

Here, at the Japanese surrender, are three of the architects of victory in the Pacific: Commander in Chief of the Pacific Fleet Admiral Chester W. Nimitz, General Douglas MacArthur (right), and behind him Admiral William Halsey.

great shortage of good pilots. These ships would be dangled off the northern end of the Philippines in the virtual certainty that Halsey would run north to get them and leave the transports and landing craft in Leyte Gulf uncovered. To annihilate these defenseless vessels and defeat the invasion, two forces were prepared. One was to fuel at Brunei Bay in Borneo, then run north and come through San Bernardino Strait north of Samar. It would comprise the best of the Japanese battleships and cruisers and be more than a match for Kinkaid's old-timers. A smaller surface force, based in Japan, was to run through Surigao Strait south of Leyte and take care of any vessels that might evade Admiral Takeo Kurita's main force.

On October 20, 1944, MacArthur landed and announced, "People of the Philippines, I have returned." The infantry started its drive to retake the islands, and then, on October 23, the greatest sea battle in history began.

This was the war's most famous photograph —the marine flag-raising on Iwo Jima.

The American submarines *Darter* and *Dace* found Kurita steaming north, sank two of his cruisers, and gave Halsey his position. Through October 24, Halsey's planes kept after Kurita and sank one of the world's two largest battleships, *Musashi,* with her 18-inch guns. Just at last light, Halsey received a report from a scout plane that Kurita was turning back from the western end of San Bernardino Strait. Satisfied that his opponent had had enough, Halsey turned and raced north to hit the Japanese carriers.

During the night, the Japanese southern force started through Surigao Strait in column and Kinkaid had them spotted. At the eastern end, he had his old battlewagons in line and waiting in the classic surface-navy tactical position: He was the crossbar on the enemy T. The Japanese saved only one destroyer out of all the ships that went into the strait.

So far, so good, but Kinkaid's force had used up most of its ammunition, and with Halsey up north, Kurita turned back and into San Bernardino Strait. Urging his force to "Advance, counting on divine assistance," he ran through the strait at night, a superb piece of navigation, and at dawn was ready to fall upon the transports, which were covered by only a small force of light carriers, three destroyers, and four little destroyer escorts. Kurita had four battleships—one the 18-inch *Yamato*—seven cruisers, and a screen of destroyers. Admiral C.A.F. Sprague, commanding the north carrier group, could only run south with his thin-skinned vessels, try to recover his aircraft—which were supporting ground troops—and get them back into the air with armor-piercing bombs. The destroyers and the destroyer escorts had to cover the retreat as best they could with torpedoes and smoke. In one of the great actions in American naval history, the seven little ships sacrificed themselves to stall the Japanese giants. Three were sunk and the others were riddled, but they stayed alive long enough for Sprague to get his planes off against the attacker. Incredibly, with victory in his hands, Kurita turned and ran back through the straits. He had heard of the disaster at Surigao and he thought he was up against much greater forces than he was, but his decision can only be recorded as one of the great blunders of the war. Up north, Halsey had knocked out four enemy carriers and the last great counterattack had failed.

It took until June, 1945, to clear the Philippines fully, but from that day on, the issue was never really in doubt. Long before that, on February 19, 1945, marines had gone ashore on the little island of Iwo Jima—the object, to get an airfield from which fighter cover could go with the B-29s against Japan and provide a way station for damaged bombers coming back. Admiral Spruance plastered the island with everything he had, but the Japanese held out against the invaders for nearly a month. There were 25,000 casualties before the job was done, and the Marine Corps declared it the toughest engagement in their history.

The last battle

There remained only the island of Okinawa, just south of Japan and an ideal staging point for an invasion of the home islands. Army troops and marines went ashore on April 1, 1945,

To avoid the casualties it would cost to invade Japan, the atomic bomb was dropped on Hiroshima. Only this was left a mile from the center of the blast.

and it looked easy. A wily Japanese commander had pulled his forces back into the hills to escape the bombardment he knew the Americans would put on the landing beaches. It took until the end of June to clear the island, and in the process, the navy took its worst pounding since Pearl Harbor. The Japanese turned to suicide pilots —kamikazes. They were half-trained, sworn to die, and flying anything that could be got off the ground. They did not even try to bomb the American ships from the air; the bomb-ladened planes simply flew straight into their targets—planes, bombs, and pilots vanishing in a last glorious blast for homeland and emperor. The navy had 36 ships sunk and 368 damaged, and back in Washington, government officials wondered how much higher the price might be when Japan itself was invaded. There was still a Japanese army of 2,500,000 men, and President Harry S. Truman—succeeding Franklin D. Roosevelt, who had died in April—pondered a bitter decision.

The B-29s had lacerated Japan, but there was still no sign of surrender. In 1939, Dr. Albert Einstein had written Roosevelt about the possibility of building an atomic bomb. It was now ready—a weapon, as President Truman told Joseph Stalin at the Potsdam Conference, "the like of which has never been seen on this earth." It was estimated that half a million American lives could be saved if the bomb could knock Japan out of the war. Truman decided to use it, and on August 6, 1945, a B-29 named *Enola Gay,* piloted by Colonel Paul Tibbets, was over the Japanese city of Hiroshima, population 343,000.

On the blinding light and the mushroom cloud that followed, the crew of the plane could make only one comment: "My God."

Something like 120,000 people were killed, obliterated, or wounded.

Three days later, a second bomb was dropped on Nagasaki. Again there was the great fireball and the huge casualties. On August 14, the Japanese Supreme War Council decided that the time had come to surrender. Fanatics still resisted, but the next day, the emperor himself went on the radio and told his people that the war was over.

On September 2, 1945, an American fleet steamed into Tokyo Bay, and while planes flew fighter cover overhead, the surrender papers were signed on deck of the battleship U.S.S. *Missouri.*

A total of some 17,000,000 servicemen on both sides had died. There can be no exact count of the number of civilian dead, but an estimate is 18,-000,000. American military casualties alone had been 1,078,674. Now the nation faced the peace uneasily, with a new President, with the question of whether the economy could absorb 15,000,000 men and women returning from service, and signs aplenty that America's wartime ally, Russia, would be no ally or even a friend in the postwar world.

UNITED NATIONS

THE UNITED NATIONS

The expression "United Nations" was first used officially in a declaration made on January 1, 1942, in which 26 nations pledged themselves to carry on the war against the Axis until the finish. (The 26 leaders, plus General Charles de Gaulle, who seemed most likely to be the future leader of France, are shown on the following pages.) The charter was drawn up at the San Francisco Conference of 1945, and in that year the U.N. became a reality, with 51 member nations. If it has not brought the universal peace that some hoped it would, it has a considerable body of achievement to its credit. Today, delegates from 110 nations pour out 13,000,000 words a year at its meetings; the talk is sometimes wearisome, but as Winston Churchill said, "Jaw, jaw, jaw is better than war, war, war." In Korea, the U.N. stood up to naked aggression far better than the old League of Nations ever did. It played a powerful role in settling the Suez crisis of 1956 and left a police force in the Gaza Strip that has tried to maintain the precarious peace there. The intervention in the Congo was the most important single event in the life of that unhappy nation. As the U.N. has grown to more than double its original membership, there has been a significant change in the balance of power. In the early days, the United States and its allies could muster a slight edge over the Soviet bloc on most issues. Today, the Afro-Asian bloc—many of its members new, small countries—has the votes in the General Assembly to overrule the supporters of either of the world's two great atomic powers. The police actions of the U.N. have been the most widely reported; in this portfolio the emphasis is on its nonmilitary activities.

THE UNITED NATIONS...FOR WAR AND FOR PEACE

A FANCIFUL ASSEMBLAGE OF THE HEADS OF STATE OF THE UNITED NATIONS
PAINTED IN 1942 BY MIGUEL COVARRUBIAS
IN THE BEST CARICATURING TRADITION OF THE FREE PRESS OF THE FREE WORLD

1 King George II of Greece

2 Grand Duchess Charlotte of the Grand Duchy of Luxembourg

3 Mackenzie King, Prime Minister of the Dominion of Canada

4 Generalissimo Chiang Kai-shek of China

5 Franklin D. Roosevelt, President of the United States of America

6 Winston Churchill, Prime Minister of the United Kingdom of Great Britain and Northern Ireland

7 Joseph Stalin, Chairman of the Council of People's Commissars of the Union of Soviet Socialist Republics

8 Queen Wilhelmina of the Netherlands

9 General Tiburcio Carias Andino, President of Honduras

10 King Haakon VII of Norway

11 King Peter II of Yugoslavia

12 John Curtin, Prime Minister of Australia

13 Peter Fraser, Prime Minister of New Zealand

14 General Wladyslaw Sikorski, Prime Minister of Poland

15 Hubert Pierlot, Prime Minister of Belgium

16 Eduard Benes, President of the Czechoslovak Republic

17 General Jan C. Smuts, Prime Minister of the Union of South Africa

18 Fulgencio Batista, President of Cuba

19 General Anastasio Somoza, President of Nicaragua

20 The Marquis of Linlithgow, Viceroy of India

21 Elie Lescot, President of Haiti

22 Ricardo Adolfo de la Guardia, President of Panama

23 Dr. Manuel de Jesus Troncoso de la Concha, President of the Dominican Republic

24 Dr. Rafael Angel Calderon Guardia, President of Costa Rica

25 General Maximiliano H. Martinez, President of El Salvador

26 General Jorge Ubico Castañeda, President of Guatemala

27 General Charles de Gaulle of the Free French

THE HOME OFFICE

DICK HANLEY, PHOTO RESEARCHERS

The home of the United Nations is at the edge of New York City's East River. The lower building in the foreground (right) houses the General Assembly and the special councils. The taller shaft to the rear, with glass sides and marble ends, is the office building for the Secretariat—the permanent professional staff of the organization. Various nations have contributed ornamentation; paradoxically, the muscular figure beating his sword into a plowshare (left) is a gift of the bellicose Soviet bloc. When the General Assembly is in session, flags of all member nations are displayed (below). These meetings begin each September and, after a midwinter break, continue into March or April.

ELLIOTT ERWITT, MAGNUM

RUSS KINNE, PHOTO RESEARCHERS

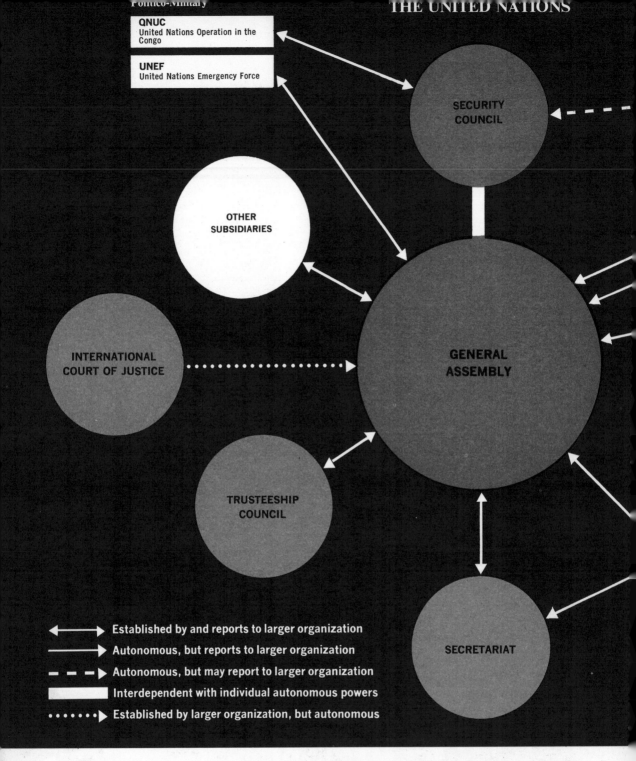

QNUC
United Nations Operation in the Congo

UNEF
United Nations Emergency Force

SECURITY
COUNCIL

OTHER
SUBSIDIARIES

INTERNATIONAL
COURT OF JUSTICE

GENERAL
ASSEMBLY

TRUSTEESHIP
COUNCIL

SECRETARIAT

Established by and reports to larger organization
Autonomous, but reports to larger organization
Autonomous, but may report to larger organization
Interdependent with individual autonomous powers
Established by larger organization, but autonomous

The General Assembly and the Security Council are the heart of the U.N. All member nations of the Assembly have one vote each. It is charged with a number of functions, the chief one being "to discuss any problem affecting peace and security." The Security Council has five permanent members—Nationalist China, France, Russia, the United Kingdom, and the United States. There are six additional members, each elected for two years by the General Assembly. The Council is charged with even more responsibility than the Assembly; its chief function is to "maintain international peace and security."

IAEA
International Atomic Energy Agency

SPECIALIZED AGENCIES

ILO
International Labor Organization

FAO
Food and Agriculture Organization
of the United Nations

UNESCO
United Nations Educational, Scientific
and Cultural Organization

WHO
World Health Organization

ICAO
International Civil Aviation Organization

UPU
Universal Postal Union

ITU
International Telecommunication Union

WMO
World Meteorological Organization

IFC
International Finance Corporation

IBRD
International Bank for Reconstruction
and Development

IDA
International Development Association

IMF
International Monetary Fund

IMCO
Inter-Governmental Maritime
Consultative Organization

ICITO—GATT
Interim Commission for the International Trade
Organization—General Agreement on Tariffs and Trade

Socio-Economic

UNRWA
United Nations Relief and Works
Agency for Palestine Refugees

UNHCR
Office of United Nations High
Commissioner for Refugees

United Nations Special Fund

UNICEF
United Nations Children's Fund

TAB
Technical
Assistance
Board

**ECONOMIC AND
SOCIAL COUNCIL**

The other major organizations of the United Nations are the International Court of Justice, the Trusteeship Council, Secretariat, and the Economic and Social Council. The court is the U.N.'s principal judicial body. The Trusteeship Council stands guard over underdeveloped areas on their way to self-government. The Secretariat is the dominion of the Secretary-General and his staff of about 4,000. The Economic and Social Council oversees an enormous variety of technical-assistance and cultural programs. This chart was drawn especially for this portfolio by Richard Hendler and is based on information obtained at the United Nations.

THE HEART

When the General Assembly is in session, the Secretary-General and his staff members sit at the far right (above) under the great seal. At the left is one of the two large Fernand Leger murals that decorate the chamber. The delegates (right) have a choice of hearing a speech translated into either English, French, Spanish, Chinese, or Russian. The same simultaneous translation takes place in the Security Council (left), where the mural is a gift to the U.N. from Norway. Only the five permanent members of the Security Council have the veto power.

UNITED NATIONS

THE UNITED NATIONS

BRANCH OFFICES

The U.N. ranges far from New York City. The International Court of Justice sits at The Hague in the Netherlands (above). Its 15 judges are elected by the Security Council and the General Assembly; care is taken to see that all the leading legal systems of the world are represented. The old League of Nations building at Geneva (right, above) contains many of the U.N. European offices. Of all the U.N. multinational efforts, intervention in Korea was the greatest. Soldiers (right) of 16 nations participated in the three-year struggle and suffered some 400,000 casualties.

THE UNITED NATIONS

IN NEWEST AFRICA

An important part of the U.N. activities has been to assist nations that have just attained independence or are about to do so. Above, youngsters celebrate the new Republic of Rwanda, which had been a part of the territory—Ruanda-Urundi—administered by Belgium for the Trusteeship Council. In the Congo, the U.N. faced a hornet's nest of problems, which have still to be settled. Secretary-General Dag Hammarskjold died in an air crash in Africa while trying to resolve some of them. One problem was displaced natives, whom the U.N. fed and then sent back to their own lands. At the right, members of the Baluba tribe crowd around an official while he announces over a loud-speaker those who are about to be taken home.

MEDICAL AID

UNICEF—the United Nations Children's Fund—is one of the most important subbodies of the Economic and Social Council. Formed originally to bring immediate aid to child victims of World War II, its activities have been expanded to take in the long-term needs of children. Working particularly in underdeveloped areas, it deals in both direct disease control and educational programs aimed at better child and maternity care. At the left, a medical team in Morocco examines children for trachoma, which can cause blindness. At the right, doctors in Indonesia examine for yaws, and below, powdered milk is being distributed to Masai tribesmen in Kenya.

UNICEF

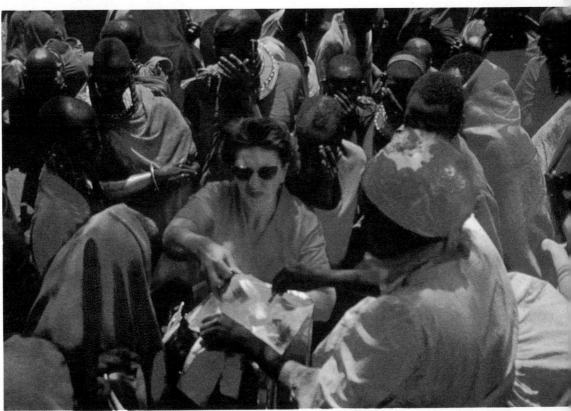

UNITED NATIONS

UNICEF

BOOKS AND CLASSES

The intergovernmental agencies related to the United Nations cooperate with the U.N. but are not directly a part of it. Indeed, some of them—like the International Telecommunications Union, which was founded in 1865—existed long before the U.N. itself. Their activities are financed by the member governments, but the U.N. Technical Assistance Board serves as a coordinating agency for their work. At the right, a horse-drawn library sponsored by UNESCO —the United Nations Educational, Scientific and Cultural Organization—has just arrived in a Thailand village. Below, Peruvian villagers vote on a proposition put by a UNESCO rural-education expert. He trains them not only in technical skills, but helps them gain practical experience in self-government at the local level. Below, right, a Food and Agricultural Organization instructor from the Netherlands teaches Congolese natives how to use a tractor at a farm school in Leopoldville, the capital.

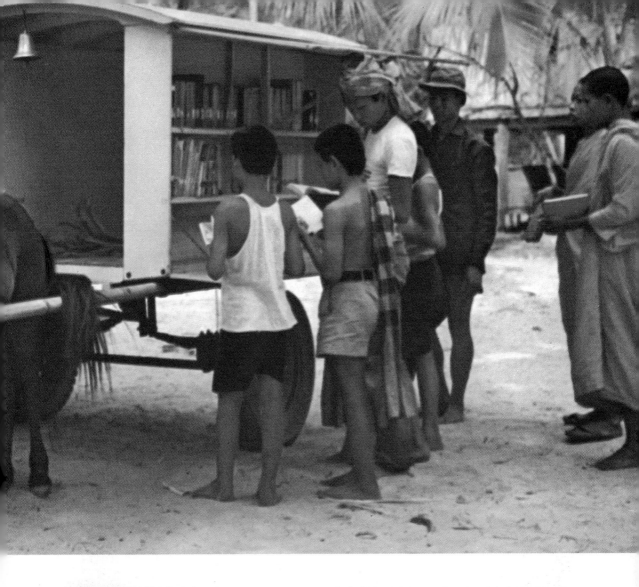

ALL: UNITED NATIONS

NEW FRONTIERS

In addition to its medical and instructional programs, the U.N. also offers economic assistance, both direct and indirect. The yarn merchant at the left is an Arab refugee living in the Gaza Strip whom the U.N. Works Agency helped set up in business. The aqueduct below is part of a Japanese irrigation project, which was helped along by a World Bank loan of nearly $5,000,000. The aqueduct will not only bring new acres under cultivation to enlarge Japan's food supply, but will also supply, for the first time, adequate drinking water for many small villages in the area. The U.N. provides help, too, for local farmers learning how best to use new projects like the irrigation canal at the right in West Pakistan.

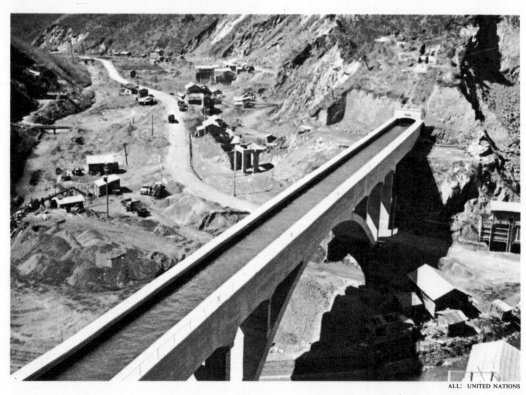

ALL: UNITED NATIONS

Today the U.N. still fights, as its charter specifies, "to save succeeding generations from the

scourge of war . . . to promote social progress and better standards of life in larger freedom."

1332

CHAPTER 45

THE HOME AND DIPLOMATIC FRONTS

In a conflict that had lasted six years, the dictators Hitler, Mussolini, and Tojo had been defeated by the combined forces of Churchill, Roosevelt, and Stalin. Throughout, Roosevelt and Churchill had conferred often—starting with the Atlantic Charter meeting in 1941. They met again at Casablanca in January, 1943, with Charles de Gaulle present, and in November at Cairo along with Chiang Kai-shek of China. Finally, later in November, the Big Three met together for the first time at Teheran, Iran. The conference was marked by military planning, a reaffirmation of the fact that the Allies planned a world organization after the war, and a vast number of pronouncements of good-fellowship spurred on by endless toasts.

Then in February, 1945, with the conflict drawing to an end, the Big Three met again, this time at the Russian Black Sea resort of Yalta, for the

The Big Three meet at Yalta with Churchill, Roosevelt, and Stalin. Sir Anthony Eden, Edward R. Stettinius, Jr., Sir Alexander Cadogan, Vyacheslav Molotov, and Averell Harriman are behind them. Yalta became the most controversial wartime conference.

most controversial gathering of the war. In the years following, Roosevelt would be accused of being duped.

The facts are somewhat less melodramatic. It would be well to realize Roosevelt's aims at Yalta. He wanted Russia to enter the war against Japan at a time when that nation was still strong and an invasion of the Japanese home islands threatened untold casualties. Like Woodrow Wilson before him, he wanted a postwar association of nations and, like Wilson, he was willing to make certain concessions to get it.

What was actually done at Yalta? A date was set for the San Francisco conference that would charter the United Nations. Russia would enter the war against Japan, but her entry had a big price tag on it: She was to get back all the territory she had lost to Japan in the Russo-Japanese War and was also to have the Kurile Islands, which had always been Japanese. The autonomy of the Mongolian People's Republic, which had existed since 1924, was recognized, although China still claimed the area as the Chinese province of Outer Mongolia. Chiang Kai-shek

In this Persian miniature commemorating the Teheran Conference, Stalin, Churchill, Roosevelt, and Chiang (left to right) hunt down Mussolini, Hitler, and Tojo. The artist, Haji Musavirel Mulk, made one for Churchill, one for F.D.R.

was not informed, and Roosevelt was assigned to break the news to him. In Eastern Europe, some minor adjustments were made in the Polish-Russian border, but it remained basically as it was established by the Allies after World War I.

The most bitterly contested decision concerned the Polish government. The Russians, in military occupation of Poland, naturally favored a group that was Communist-oriented. The British and Americans favored another Polish government, in exile in London. It was agreed that the Russian-backed group should be enlarged

to include some of the Londoners, and the eventual government chosen by the Poles themselves in a free election. It can certainly be said that Roosevelt misread Stalin badly if he thought the dictator would ever permit truly free elections in a Russian-occupied country.

Considering the time at which the Yalta Conference was held, the agreements contained some good judgment and some bad. After the war, when quarreling among recent allies disillusioned the free world, it was much easier, with hindsight, to show up some of the decisions for the mistakes they were and to blame those who made them.

The final great conference of the war was held at Potsdam, Germany, in July, 1945. One member of the Big Three was new; Roosevelt was dead and Harry S. Truman had replaced him. Churchill represented England at first, but before the end, he had been voted out of office and replaced by Labor Prime Minister Clement R. Attlee. The conference was largely concerned with Stalin's demanding and getting huge reparations from Germany in return for the enormous damage his nation had suffered.

The home front

Although the United States raised an armed force of unprecedented size, less than 15% of the population was actually in uniform. For most people, the war was something one read about, heard about on the radio, or saw either in heavily edited or censored newsreels or in unrealistic mov-

The Potsdam Conference ended with a new team representing the Allies—Clement R. Atlee, Harry S. Truman, and Joseph Stalin. Behind them are Admiral William D. Leahy, Britain's Ernest Bevin, James F. Byrnes, and Vyacheslav Molotov.

A wartime poster lauds the support of the women at home who went to work in factories to help keep the supply lines filled.

ies in which handfuls of Americans decimated three times as many Japanese. There actually were merchant-ship sinkings within sight of East Coast residents and the Japanese did attempt to set fire to West Coast forests, but no bombs fell on American soil. Most citizens assumed, in one way or another, the role of the man behind the man behind the gun. Yet nearly everyone was personally involved, usually through a father, son, daughter, or other relative in service. Some worked in defense industries, others volunteered for a wide vari-

ety of duties, including those of air-raid wardens, auxiliary firemen, and aircraft-warning watchers, and the thankless jobs of ration-board clerk or draft-board member.

Although Selective Service included men between 45 and 65, with the idea of a possible labor draft, no such legislation was necessary. American labor produced as never before and with a minimum of complaint. The picture, however, was not completely unmarred by strikes. Part of the trouble came from antilabor legislation passed by Congress, which helped to induce just what it tried to avoid. Workers wanted to retain all the gains they had made during the early days of the New Deal, and they feared that restrictions imposed in wartime might be kept in force afterward.

In June, 1943, apprehensive Congressmen passed the War Labor Disputes Act over Roosevelt's veto. It empowered the President to take over any industry threatened by stoppage through labor disputes. The Congressmen were unduly jittery. The loss of man-hours through strikes during the war was less than from absenteeism in the same businesses or industries in peacetime.

The vast war was expensive, costing the United States $330,500,000,000 compared to $41,755,000,000 for its predecessor in 1917–18. Industrial mobilization followed the pattern worked out in the later stages of World War I. The highest authority was the War Production Board, and workers came under the War Manpower Commission. Other agencies, such as the War Shipping Administration, the War Food Administration, and the Foreign Economic Administration, guided and correlated the nation's resources.

In some cases there was little to conserve or allocate. Raw rubber, for example, was almost nonexistent, as Japan controlled about 90% of the world's supply shortly after Pearl Harbor. The United States had less than a year's supply at the outbreak of hostilities. This was impressed sharply on the people at home when in January, 1942, a strict rationing of tires and other rubber products was put in force. The ever-present sight of balding tires was a constant reminder to automobile-conscious America that a real crisis was at hand. Gasoline rationing and a national speed limit of 35 miles an hour underscored it.

Production problems of all kinds faced the nation, but one of the most important was coordination as automobile and threshing-machine factories turned to producing tanks and airplanes.

After some preliminary difficulties, the job went well. A Congressional watchdog committee headed by Senator Harry S. Truman (Democrat, Missouri) assumed the task of shepherding the laggards, investigating charges of excess profits, and cutting away obstacles that impeded production schedules. In the process, it made such a name for its chairman that he

The driver of a barouche in New York City's Central Park gets a horse laugh with a newspaper announcing gas rationing.

was the Democratic nominee for Vice-President in the 1944 elections.

By 1942, American war production was equal to that of the Axis powers, and by 1944 it far surpassed their combined effort. The various controls imposed on industry and the consumer would normally have been resented as socialistic, but in the emergency, most of those who stayed at home submitted to unusual disciplines with reasonably good grace.

Early in 1942, the Office of Price Administration was established to fix what it regarded as a fair price on

1337

food items and thus attempt to prevent runaway inflation. Early efforts to keep prices stable were only partly successful, and by the spring of 1943, Roosevelt was forced to issue his "hold the line" order that price-fixed almost every item in the economy. It was so effective that in the next two years, price rises were held to 2%. During the whole war, prices rose approximately 30%, an increase about half that of the 1914–18 period.

Materially, the American people sacrificed but did not suffer. Although the purchasing power of the dollar declined slightly due to inflation, the nation enjoyed full employment for the first time since the '20s.

The return of peace

Franklin D. Roosevelt died on April 12, 1945, after serving a little over 12 years in the White House. That evening the Vice-President, Harry S. Truman, was sworn in as his successor. Just as Lincoln had died on an April day at the very climax of a successful war, so Roosevelt passed away in his moment of triumph. Truman, like Lincoln's successor Andrew Johnson before him, was faced with the thorny task of making the peace.

Truman, a crisp-speaking and sometimes jaunty Missourian, was better prepared for what lay ahead than many of his contemporaries knew. A story made the rounds that in the summer of 1944, Roosevelt revealed to a Washington figure that Truman was to be his running mate in the election that year. The recipient of the news is said to have replied, "Who the hell is Harry Truman?" Not everyone was so ill-informed. The new President had served in the Senate since 1934. His fairness and capacity for hard work had favorably impressed the public.

Still, America faced the peace led

Vice-President Truman, left, dines with F.D.R. at Warm Springs. His record as the head of the Senate watchdog committee on war production won him the job.

Franklin Roosevelt rides through Washington for the last time. The nation mourned as the President's body traveled from Georgia to Hyde Park, New York.

by a man inexperienced in the massive complexities of global affairs. The ancient territorial ambitions of Russia, now strengthened by an ideology that promised them eventual victory over the capitalistic West, were making themselves felt. Europe lay in ruins, and it was clear that the means to rebuild it would have to come largely from the United States. In Asia there was turmoil as nations threw off old colonial bonds, and even in 1945 there were signs of the gravest weaknesses in Chiang Kai-shek's government in China.

At home, the largest armed force that America had ever assembled had to be dispersed, and there were great pressures to do it rapidly. Both civilians and servicemen clamored for immediate demobilization. Early in 1946, there were riots among some troops abroad that did not think the government was moving fast enough. Goaded by such pressures, Congress cut the fighting forces as quickly as it could. The naysayers muttered direly about a "mature economy" and questioned whether jobs could be found for all those returning. The man in the White House and the people he led faced a future that threatened to be nearly as troublesome as the period through which they had just passed.

MAIN TEXT CONTINUES IN VOLUME 16

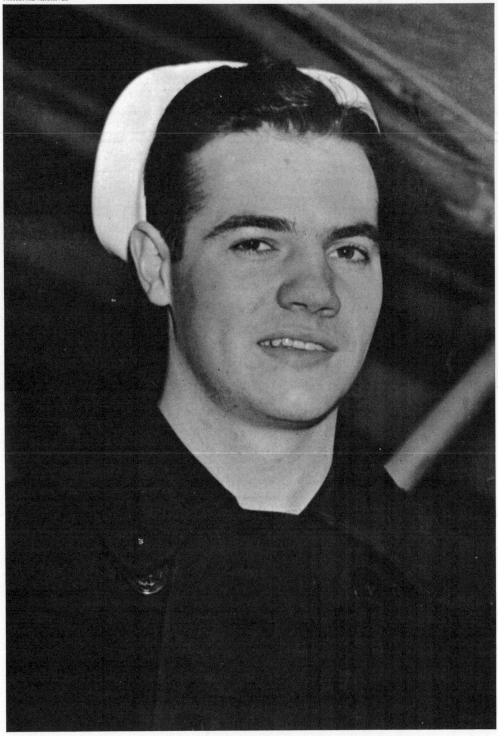

Gunner's mate second class Allen Heyn was one of the 10 men out of more than 700 aboard the cruiser U.S.S. Juneau *who survived her sinking.*

One Who Survived:
The Narrative of Allen Heyn

Day after day, the sun, the sea, and the sharks cut down the men who clung to a doughnut life raft, until on the ninth day a plane spotted the solitary survivor.

O f all those who have gone down to the sea in ships, few have lived to tell a more graphic story than Allen Clifton Heyn, gunner's mate second class, one of the 10 survivors of more than 700 men aboard the United States light cruiser Juneau. *This special contribution is a transcript of a recorded wartime interview between Heyn and a naval interrogator, reproduced here with permission of the Navy Department. Except for some cuts and for a few slight alterations in wording in the interest of clarity, nothing has been changed.*

ALLEN HEYN'S STORY

LT. PORTER: Heyn, you were on the *Juneau* in Guadalcanal action; that was 13 November 1942, wasn't it?

ALLEN HEYN: Yes, sir.

LT. PORTER: What was your battle station?

HEYN: I was on the 1.1 on the fantail. [A light gun at the stern.]

LT. PORTER: What did you see of the action that night?

HEYN: We were in a column of ships and we went in, in between these Japanese ships, and we got word down from the bridge to stand by, that they would challenge the enemy. And it wasn't but a few minutes when everything just broke loose, flames and shots and gunfire all over. And they sent word all around to all the minor batteries like 1.1s and 20 millimeters [antiaircraft machine guns] not to fire because the tracers would give away our positions.

So we held our fire until the enemy knew where we were and the star shells [fired to illuminate or silhouette an enemy at night] lit us all up. Then we started firing, and you could see the Jap ships so close that you'd think you could almost throw something and hit them. So we just fired our smaller guns right into the topsides [superstructures] of their ships, trying to knock off some of the guns on their decks. That went on quite a while and the ship maneuvered around a lot.

I don't know whether they knew there was a fish [torpedo] coming or what, but all at once a fish hit. It must have hit up forward because it just seemed like the fish jumped out of the water.* And when it did, all of us fellows that were on the main deck, it stunned us like and knocked us down. The propellers didn't seem to turn for a few minutes. Sounded like they were jammed or something. The ship wouldn't steer, just seemed to skid through the water like. I don't know whether it was a Jap cruiser or what it was, but it was on the other side of us and it just seemed like we were going to run right into it and ram it, but we didn't, though.

The ship seemed to be out of control, and they passed the word around to cut some of the life rafts loose. There were four or five of these doughnut rafts stacked on top of each other on the main deck aft, and they were

*It struck the forward fireroom (Samuel Eliot Morison, *The Struggle for Guadalcanal, History of U.S. Naval Operations in World War II, Vol. V*).

secured, so two or three guys from the battle station where I was went up and cut them loose with a knife and come back.

After that, things started to quiet down a little. We got out of position and didn't see any more ships around us. The forward part of the ship seemed to be way down in the water and the fantail way up high. And we couldn't make very good speed. You could hear the things cracking underneath there—the propeller shafts and the rudder. They were bent or something.

It was beginning to get daylight by then, and we got out in the open sea again. The radars and things didn't work very good; they were all shot from the explosion. Then the lookouts picked up ships ahead. They signaled recognition signals, and we found out then it was some of our own task force.

It was the *San Francisco,* the *Buchanan,* and I don't know the name of the other can. The *San Francisco* sent over word to our ship asking for a doctor and some pharmacist's mates to come over and aid them. We only had two small motor launches on the davits and they were all torn away. So they [the *San Francisco*] sent a boat over, and a doctor and I don't know how many pharmacist's mates got in. After they got there, we were always having alerts. There were planes flying around.

We were still at our battle stations and didn't know for sure what they were.

Then it was kinda quiet and it was sort of a lull for a few minutes, and everybody was kinda talking and breathing a little easy—everybody was pretty well shook up from the night before. I remember I was just relieving another man on my gun on the phones. We took turns every once in a while so it would be easier. It was pretty hard on your ears and everything, and I took over one phone. I was putting them on while he was taking the other ones off.

And I said to him, "Are you ready?" And he didn't say anything, he just looked at me, kinda with his mouth open. I didn't know what it was, somebody was passing the word over the phone or what. It just seemed like everybody was just standing there and then an explosion. A torpedo struck or something. It struck about midship because the whole thing just blew up and it threw me against a gun mount. I had one of these steel helmets on and when I came to, everything was all torn apart and there was oil coming down the air and I thought it was rain, but it was just the oil from the feed tanks or something. The tanks had blew up in the air.

And there was smoke and there was fellows laying all around there and parts of their gun shields torn apart and the fantail where I was

1342

sticking almost straight up in the air. It was so slippery that you couldn't walk up it, and the guys that was still able to climb over the side couldn't walk up. They were crawling over the side and holding on the life line trying to pull themselves further aft and jump over. And they were jumping over and bumping into each other.

It was still so smoky and all, you couldn't quite see, and I was still hazy and I knew I had to get up and get off of there. I was afraid the suction would pull me down. When I went to get up, I felt this pain in my foot and I couldn't get my foot loose from the shield or something; it fell down on top of my right foot across the instep of it and I couldn't get loose. It was only a few seconds, and the water was closing in around the ship and there was just this little bit of it left. And I knew that I had to get off but I couldn't, and there was a lot of kapok life jackets laying around deck.

I grabbed one of them in my arms and held it. I didn't even put it on, and the water closed in around the ship and we went down. And I gave up; I just thought that there wasn't a chance at all—everything just run through my head. And you could see all objects in the water, all the fellows and everything, and after we were under the surface—I don't know how far, but the sheet of iron or whatever it

The night cruiser action of November 13, 1942, began with the Japanese sending a force to bombard Guadalcanal. An American force under Admiral Daniel J. Callaghan in the San Francisco *(above, left) intercepted. The Japanese were turned back, but Admiral Callaghan was killed, and the* Juneau *and one other ship, the* Atlanta, *were sunk.*

was, it was released and my foot came loose and then the buoyancy from the life jacket brought me back to the surface.

It was like a big whirlpool. There was oil very thick on the water, it was at least two inches thick—seemed that way, anyway—and there was all kinds of blueprints and drawings of the ship floating around. And then there was roll after roll of tissue paper, and that's about all there was on top. I couldn't see anybody. I thought, gee, am I the only one here? My head was very hazy and I didn't think a thing about the other ships. I put the life jacket on when I came to the top, and I paddled around the water.

I don't know how long—it wasn't too long —when this doughnut life raft just popped right up in front of me. I don't know where it came from; it just seemed to come up there. I grabbed it and held on, and then I heard a man cry. I looked around and it was this boatswain's mate second class. His name—I can't quite remember his name. If I could see it, I'd recognize it. He was in the post office on the ship and he was crying for help. I went over to help him.

He said he couldn't swim and he had his whole leg torn off, blew off. I helped him on the doughnut raft and then gradually one by one some more stragglers would come and we'd all get on.

Everybody was kinda scared at first. Some of them couldn't swim; they were afraid they'd lose their grip and drown. So it went on that way and then these B-17 Flying Fortresses flew over the area. They just skimmed the water and they'd wave to us.*

Well, by nightfall we were about three doughnuts together. [The doughnut is a large circular float supporting a rope net, accommodating a good many partially submerged men.] It just lays on the water and you try to lay on top of it. Well, there was a lot of fellows on them. I should say there was about 140 of us when we all got together. Some of them were in very bad shape. Their arms and legs were torn off. And one of them, I could see myself his skull. You could see the red part inside where his head had been split open. They were all crying together and very down in the dumps and wondering if anybody was ever going to pick them up. And they thought, well, at least tomorrow there will be somebody out here. And that night—it was a very hard night because the fellows who were wounded badly were all in agony. And in the morning this fellow that had his head torn open, his hair had turned gray just like he was an old man. It turned gray right overnight.

The oil was so thick it sort of made everybody sick to their stomachs. So we decided to try to get out of the oil. Where the water was clear it didn't bother you so much, but then we worried because we knew there were sharks in those waters.

Then Lieutenant Blodgett—he was gunnery officer, he was a full lieutenant on the *Juneau*—he took charge of the party and he decided that we ought to try to paddle for land because we could see land when we first went down. And what we done, we secured the doughnuts together, one behind another in a line and the fellows that were able would get up in the forward ones and straddle legs over it [the floats] and paddle. And we done that all day. We took turns. All that night we done the same thing. And the lieutenant was supposed to be navigating by the stars.

Well, we didn't seem to be getting anywhere at all because the doughnuts were so clumsy. The ones who were wounded that hadn't died already had narrowed down to about 50 men. The ones of us who were in the best shape, we tried to swim around and help out the other ones. And some of the fellows—there was some planks there—they decided they'd try to swim for land on these planks. Well, they tried to do it and I never did see a couple of them again, but this one fellow came back; he found out he couldn't make it and he came back to our party on this big wooden plank.

Well, the sea began to get rough again. In the daytime the sun was very hot and I found out that the fellows who took their shirts off, or the ones that had them torn off by the explosion, their backs, their skin had all burned. And the ones of us who kept our clothes on were in the best shape because of the oil in the clothes. That protected us. At night it was very cold; you'd have to keep under the water to keep yourself warm. In the daytime the oil in the clothes would keep the sun off you, wouldn't penetrate your body so much.

But then on the fourth day the sea was very rough; the doughnuts began to separate. There were about 12 on mine. There was a gunner's mate second, his name was—it's so long ago, I'm forgetting the names of all these fellows— well anyway, there was him, there was a boat-

According to Morison's book on the Guadalcanal battles, the *Helena*, whose captain was now senior officer present, asked a Flying Fortress to notify the South Pacific command that *Juneau* had been torpedoed and that survivors were in the water, but this message did not get through. Admiral William F. Halsey, Jr., later relieved the captain of his command for abandoning the survivors. It can be argued that it was too hazardous to stop in these waters then, especially for wounded ships, but lifeboats and rafts could have been dropped.

COMBAT ART SECTION, U.S. NAVY

swain's mate and myself and this George Sullivan, he was gunner's mate second. I think he was the oldest brother of the Sullivans, he was on the raft with me. There was several others; there was a Polish fellow from somewhere in Pennsylvania. I remember him talking about he was a coal miner before the war. And then there was a fellow from Tennessee.

We tried to paddle and we found it wasn't doing no good so we decided just to lay there and hope that someone would find us.

Airplanes did fly over and some of them would come down close to us and some of them wouldn't, and after a while some of the fellows were getting very delirious and, if a few waved at a plane that went by, they'd get mad at you, say you were crazy for doing it, and not to pay any attention to the planes. They didn't want to save us and they were going to leave us there. Well, I always thought that probably there was still battles going on and they couldn't send a ship out there and if we just hung on, sometime somebody would come and get us.

They knew we were there, I knew that, so when they could send a ship, they'd come. Some of the guys was kinda disappointed and

pretty low in mind, so they sorta gave up. There's one fellow, he was a gunner's mate from the *Juneau,* second class. Well, he kept swallowing salt water all the time and he'd let his head fall down in the water and swallow it and he'd begin to get very dopey and dreary. He couldn't help himself at all, so I held him up. I held him in my arms, his head above the water as much as I could, and I held him that way all afternoon. Towards night he got stiff and I told the other fellows.

I said, "Well, how about holding him a while? I can't hold him, I've got all to do to hold myself." And they said they wouldn't do it, they were arguing and fighting among themselves a lot. And I said, "I felt his heart and his wrists and I couldn't feel any beating." I figured he was dead and I said to them, "Well, I'm going to let him go."

And George Sullivan, the oldest brother of the Sullivans, he said to me, "You can't do that," he said. "It's against all regulations of the navy. You can't bury a man at sea without having official orders from some captain or the Navy Department or something like that." And I knew he was delirious and there was something wrong with him and all, but the

In this drawing of a rescue operation, a destroyer picks up men adrift in doughnut life rafts similar to the one in which Heyn floated for nine days.

other fellows, they wouldn't let me let him go.

I said to them, "Well, you hold him," and they wouldn't hold him. So it went on that way for a little while. His legs were hanging down in the water a little way below mine when a shark bit his leg, bit his leg right off below the knee. He didn't move or say anything. That was enough for me. I figured, well, I'm going to drop him. There isn't any sense holding a dead man. So we took his dog tag off, this one fellow did, and said a prayer for him and let him float away.

At night it was so cold for the fellows who didn't have no clothes, we'd try to huddle them among us to keep them warm under the water. The sharks kept getting worse in the daytime, and you could see them around us all the time. We'd kick them with our feet and splash the water and they'd keep away. But at night you'd get drowsy and you'd kinda fall asleep and you wouldn't see them coming. As night went on, they'd come and they'd grab a guy every once in a while and bite him. And once they did, they wouldn't eat him altogether, they'd just take a piece of him and go away and then they'd come back and get him and drag him away and drown him. He'd scream and holler and everything, but there wasn't anything we could do.

And then the fellows got kind of ideas that the ship was sunk under us, sitting on the bottom. You could swim down there at night and get something to eat and all them kinda things, and I was beginning to believe them. Then one night they said we were carrying ammunition from one of the forward mounts back aft and, I don't know, they said they could see a light down there and this one fellow kept saying, "If it's down there, what are we staying up here for, let's go down there and get something to eat then." So I said, "You show me the way down there." So he dives under water and I went after him and I never did find nothing down there, no hatch or anything like he said was there. And then I got my sense again and I knew what I was doing and I didn't believe him any more.

The fifth day was coming up then. Things were getting pretty bad. The guys were fighting among themselves. If you bumped into one of them, he'd get mad and holler at you. And they did talk a lot about home and what they were going to do, and a lot of them said if they could get on an island, they'd stay there, they'd never go back to the navy. They didn't want to see it no more.

Well, this day the water was calm, and it was very hot. And the fellows that didn't have shirts on, the sun burned them something awful. It burned their skin all out, and their back, it was just like as if you shaved them with a razor or something, all raw and some of them just decided, they weren't going to try any more. They said they'd rather drown themselves than suffer like that. So that night after dark George Sullivan said he was going to take a bath. And he took off all his clothes and got away from the doughnut a little way and the white of his body must have flashed and showed up more because a shark came and grabbed him and that was the end of him. I never seen him again.

Towards morning, it was rough again and the waves were high and heavy. We were getting very hungry and it started drizzling rain. A sea gull flew around and it landed on our doughnut. We grabbed at him and we missed. Then he come back and that time we caught him and wrung his neck. There was about three or four of us, I don't remember for sure, and we ate the sea gull. There wasn't much of it.

Well, another night went on and the next day, this gunner's mate second, his name was Stewart, he said that there was a hospital ship there and we were going to go over to it. There was three of us—him, me and another fellow —and he said that we should swim over to it and leave the doughnut. We didn't know whether to or not. You hated to leave it there because you knew if you got out in the water, you were gone. So he dove in the water and swam off and he just kept swimming out over the water and he wouldn't turn around. You could see the sharks going after him and he swam and kicked and swam. And he hollered to us to come and get him with the raft, to paddle towards him but he kept swimming the other way. We paddled towards him and

The five Sullivan brothers—Joseph, Francis, Albert, Madison, and George—were all lost when the Juneau *went down. A destroyer was later named after them.*

finally he got tired. He turned around and came towards us and he got back before the sharks got him.

But that night it got cold again. He had thrown all his clothes away and he didn't have a thing and he wanted me to give him my clothes. But I said no, there's no sense to that. And he said, "Well, then I'm going down to the ship and get a clean suit. I got a lot of them in my locker." He also said, "I got a case of peaches in my gun mount."

He was really thinking the ship was down there. I wouldn't let him go because I knew if he dove down into the water something would happen to him. So I kept talking him out of it. And I kept him in between us to keep him warm. Well, that night he decided he wouldn't stand it no more. He just swam away and the sharks got him.

Well, then there was just the two of us left. And it was about the seventh day or so. We talked a lot that day together and I remember I gave my knife to this Mexican boy. He was trying to secure the raft again on his end. We were at each end with our feet kinda up in the water so we could fight the sharks off better. That night we got kinda sleepy and we dozed off I guess, because a shark grabbed him and tore his leg off below, just jaggedy like. And

he complained, he said to me that somebody was stabbing him with a knife. I said, "How can anybody stab you out here? There's nobody but us two."

And he swore at me and called me all kinds of names and said I had to get him to a doctor. I guess I was delirious, because I was paddling and paddling in the water there. I didn't know where I was going. I was just paddling, trying to get him to a doctor. Well, finally he screamed and hollered and he came over to me and I held his arm and then I could see what it was. I knew that he had been bit by a shark and I held him and the shark came up and it just grabbed him underneath and kept eating him from the bottom and pulling on him. Well, I couldn't hold him any more. The sharks just pulled him down under the water and he drowned. Well then, that's all that happened. It seemed like the night would never end.

The next day I just floated around some more, and it went on like that for the next couple of days and in the morning of the last day, which was the ninth day, I began to get delirious myself. I see these guys come up out of the water. It looked like to me that they had rifles on their backs and I'd holler to them

1347

and they said they were up there on guard duty. They'd come up from each hatch on the ship. Well, I asked them how it was. And they said the ship was all right, you could go down there and get something dry and eat. So I said to them, well, I'll come over there by you and go down with you. Well, I swam over to them and they just disappeared. I went back. I done that twice. Each time they disappeared when I got there. And then my head got clear and something told me just to hang on a little longer.

And about noontime that day a PBY [Catalina seaplane] flew over and circled around and then it went away again. Well, I gave up. I figured, well, I guess it's just like all the other planes, they ain't gonna bother; they figure you ain't worth while coming for. Or maybe they didn't know what I was because I was all black. I might have been a Jap for all they knew. A couple of hours later they come back and they flew around me and they dropped smoke bombs all around me.

Well, that built up my hope a lot and I took off my shirt and I waved at them and they waved back at me and then they went off and I could see them way off flying. And I figured, well, they must be guiding the ship to me. And that's what they were doing because it wasn't long before I could see the mast of a ship coming over the horizon and it was the U.S.S. *Ballard* [a destroyer]. They lowered a small boat and came out and picked me up and that's about all, for I went on there into sick bay.

[Heyn recalls that he was rescued on November 22, 1942. He was delirious when he was taken aboard the *Ballard,* suffering from shock, exhaustion, and a broken foot. Eventually he was brought to Fiji, where he spent nine months in a naval hospital.]

Lt. Porter: Think you're fully recovered?

Heyn: I think I'm all right.

Lt. Porter: Good. Having fully recovered, you then asked for and were given submarine service. Is that right?

Heyn: Yes, that's right.

Lt. Porter: And you went out on a war patrol?

Heyn: Yes, sir.

Lt. Porter: And on that patrol, you're officially credited with sinking some five ships and damaging four?

Heyn: That's correct.

Lt. Porter: Your preference for future service would be in submarines?

Heyn: Yes, sir, it would.

Lt. Porter: Back in the same hunting area?

Heyn: It wouldn't make any difference as long as it's out in the Pacific somewhere.

This is the Heyn family at their home near Detroit, Michigan, in a recent photograph—Allen's mother, his wife Nancy, Allen, Jeffrey, Marsha, and Steven.

FOR FURTHER READING

Bailey, Thomas Aldrich. *The Man in the Street*. New York: Macmillan, 1948. The relation between American public opinion and American foreign policy.

Churchill, Winston. *The Second World War*. 6 volumes. London: Cassell, 1948–53. A penetrating interpretation of the war by a leading participant.

Eisenhower, Dwight D. *Crusade in Europe*. Garden City: Doubleday, 1948. General Eisenhower narrates his military experiences as Supreme Commander of Allied Expeditionary Forces. He covers the period from the time he left the Philippines at the end of 1940 to the postwar occupation of Germany.

Feis, Herbert. *The Road to Pearl Harbor*. Princeton: Princeton University Press. 1950. A history of Japanese-American diplomatic relations during the '30s.

Goldman, Eric. *The Crucial Decade: America, 1945–1955*. New York: Knopf, 1956. A cinematic view of the postwar decade by a leading historian.

Janeway, Eliot. *The Struggle for Survival: A Chronicle of Economic Mobilization in World War II*. New Haven: Yale University Press, 1951. A caustic summary of the administrative attitude toward domestic economic problems during World War II.

Johnson, Walter. *The Battle Against Isolation*. Chicago: University of Chicago Press, 1944. The movement toward American participation in World War II.

Langer, William L. and Sarell Everett Gleason. *The Challenge to Isolation, 1937–1940*. New York: Harpers, 1952. The response of American foreign policy to world crises. Abundantly detailed. *The Undeclared War, 1940–1941*. New York: Harpers, 1953. The conquest of Europe by the Axis powers, and Hitler's onslaught in Russia. Extensively documented.

McWilliams, Carey. *Prejudice: The Japanese-Americans*. Boston: Little, Brown, 1944. The unfortunate story of the imprisonment of thousands of Japanese-Americans on the West Coast during World War II.

Morison, Samuel Eliot. *History of Naval Operations in World War II*. 15 volumes. Boston: Little, Brown, 1947–58. A monumental history of naval operations by the United States Navy's official historian.

Pratt, Fletcher. *War for the World*. New Haven: Yale University Press, 1950. A concise narrative of American military participation in both the European and Pacific theaters.

Rauch, Basil. *Roosevelt from Munich to Pearl Harbor: A Study in the Creation of a Foreign Policy*. New York: Creative Age Press, 1950. The title is self-explanatory.

Schroeder, Paul W. *The Axis Alliance and Japanese-American Relations*, 1941. Ithaca: Cornell University Press, 1958. A useful study of the influence that the Axis powers had on Japanese-American problems.

Stein, Charles W. *The Third Term Tradition*. New York: Columbia University Press, 1943. A brief analysis of the 1940 election.

Zornow, William Frank. *America at Mid-Century*. Cleveland: Allen, 1959. A look at the Truman and Eisenhower administrations.

THE AMERICAN HERITAGE NEW ILLUSTRATED HISTORY OF THE UNITED STATES

PUBLISHED BY DELL PUBLISHING CO., INC.

George T. Delacorte, Jr., *Publisher* Helen Meyer, *President*
William F. Callahan, Jr., *Executive Vice-President*

Walter B. J. Mitchell, Jr., *Project Director;* Ross Claiborne, *Editorial Consultant;* William O'Gorman, *Editorial Assistant;* John Van Zwienen, *Art Consultant;* Rosalie Barrow, *Production Manager*

CREATED AND DESIGNED BY THE EDITORS OF AMERICAN HERITAGE MAGAZINE

James Parton, *Publisher;* Joseph J. Thorndike, Jr., *Editorial Director;* Bruce Catton, *Senior Editor;* Oliver Jensen, *Editor;* Richard M. Ketchum, *Editor, Book Division;* Irwin Glusker, *Art Director*

ROBERT R. ENDICOTT, *Project Editor-in-Chief*

James Kraft, *Assistant Editor;* Nina Page, Evelyn H. Register, Lynn Marett, *Editorial Assistants;* Lina Mainiero, *Copy Editor;* Murray Belsky, *Art Director;* Eleanor A. Dye, *Designer;* John Conley, *Assistant*